Better Life

Powerful Tips on How to Thrive by
Finding Your Focus on a Healthier,
Wealthier, Loving, and Happier You

Arun Thaploo

ISBN-13: 978-1530249503
ISBN-10: 1530249503

Dedication

Dedicated to you, the reader

Please share with your friends

Your FREE gift

I want to show my gratitude for supporting my work. Therefore, I want to give you a gift.

Email me at contactarunthaploo@gmail.com and I will send you a gift as soon as I can. You will receive your gift as a PDF file.

In addition, get notified when I release new books. You will also be notified of occasional special offers on various books and resources.

Table of Contents

Introduction

From time immemorial, some people who have experienced challenges in life have wanted to spare others the pain of having to go through what they did. As a business coach, I am often able to "get through" to my clients to help them live a life with fewer regrets. This is not always the case. My advice and hope for them are all that remain. However, my sincerest wish is that a word, a phrase, or an idea in the information I provide casts a light on something revelatory.

I wrote this book to share some of my experiences and knowledge as a business coach. Knowledge is the key to so many decisions we make in life. Making informed decisions in one's personal and professional life can minimize the number of mistakes we make along the way, both intentionally and unintentionally. The goal is to reflect over your life when you are older and experience a sense of fulfillment and satisfaction from it. It is hearing yourself say, "I've led an amazing life." Best of all, it is about realizing that it is not just about you. It is also about leaving a legacy for others to imitate, perpetuating a "pay it forward" ethic that never stops giving.

Leading an extraordinary life is the result of taking everyday circumstances and putting them to work in ways that serve you. This is the reason I am about to offer tips for having an extraordinary personal and professional life in this quick-read book. Each nugget consists of a headline followed by short "*How* and *Why*" paragraphs. This list is far from comprehensive, but it is a start. I have tried to distill some important elements from a host of ideas as well as several universally proven facts. My goal is for you to find useful information to put into immediate practice. You may know some of these tips already, but it is my conviction that you might also learn something new. And that would be my greatest reward.

Of course, there is so much material to cover—far more than what I can include in this book. That is why I hope you will stay tuned for a series of books covering individual topics in detail. Anecdotes about real people are one of the best ways to illustrate a point. For this reason, I will use exercises and true stories throughout those books. You may feel as if you are the character in many of my stories. I hope this enables you to learn how to look for pitfalls in advance and how to avoid them. The fact that you have read this far means you, like many others, are in search of ways to lead a more fulfilled life. This is the reason it is important for you to try to experience what I suggest in my exercises. After all, you have *nothing* to lose.

This book consists of seven chapters on the following topics:

1) Thinking and Creativity

2) Health and Wellness

3) Career Success

4) Family and Relationships

5) Finances and Retirement Planning

6) Communication and Influencing Skills

7) Philanthropy and Social Cause

Some tips are relevant to more than one chapter, and I repeat them along the way. I would recommend to first skim through all the tips highlighted in **bold**. In the second read-through, you should read the tips along with the *how* and *why* descriptions.

So let us begin.

Chapter One: Thinking and Creativity

"Very little is needed to make a happy life; it is all within yourself, in your way of thinking."
–Marcus Aurelius

If we have the right thinking, we can make fewer mistakes in life. Our life is the summation of all the thoughts and actions that we take along the way. We were not born with a life manual in our hands. As children, we get our thinking from our parents, teachers, friends and relatives, and the people associated with us. If we develop empowering thoughts and a positive mindset at a young age, it will help us immensely as we get older. We will be on a strong footing to face the challenges that life throws at us.

We should also pay attention to developing an artistic brain. Creative people have an inimitable way of looking at a problem. Some of their focus areas include unconventional methods of problem solving, new discoveries, inventions, innovations, and imagination. Sometimes they see something intangible that is a complete enigma from the average person's viewpoint. Creative people have better cognitive skills during old age as well.

So let us cut to the chase and move on to the tips.

1) Develop a positive outlook toward life and banish pessimism.

Try to look at the positive side of things. Even if circumstances sometimes strike you down or you fail in your endeavors, do not give up. Just fight back and beat the odds. Remember, there is nothing stronger than you; not one single problem that you are facing. Read motivational books and autobiographies of people who have overcome extreme adversity, and talk to people who bounced back in life after hard knocks.

There is a saying, "Thoughts are things. We become what we think about." If you have positive thoughts and a positive outlook on life, you have the possibility of overcoming most of life's challenges. On the contrary, if you have disempowering thoughts and you repeatedly think in a negative manner, it will have an adverse impact on the quality of your life.

2) Think ahead to prepare for the future.

Set aside at least 15 minutes every day for future planning and reflection. As another option, you can take small chunks of time every day, when you are doing nothing else but thinking. It will help you in looking at the big picture. Always have a journal, smartphone, tablet, or computer to take notes. Write down your trepidations and contemplate about them. Ask yourself: Can I do something different? What if I do this? What if I do that? Write down all possible outcomes and give due consideration to the best choices.

Thinking ahead of the present moment will help you make a predictive analysis. Our problems in life occur because of our ignorance, shortsightedness, or poor thinking. You need to think five to ten years ahead of the present time as well. Once you do this, your brain is going to throw dozens of questions at you. Do not worry; just take notes, acknowledge your thoughts, and come up with some answers. This way, you will find a solution to a problem and prepare yourself for future challenges. You will have to accept that you will not be able to predict all outcomes accurately.

3) Develop a razor-sharp memory for greater productivity and success.

Learn the tricks of remembering what is important to you. One of the best ways to do that is always being mindful about things and events happening around you. Eat foods that are good for your memory. Exercise, play outdoor games, and smile more often. Try to keep fewer thoughts in your mind at any given moment, and know how to relax and sleep well.

There is no such thing as a good memory or a bad memory. It is a subjective topic. We believe in what other people say about memory—that as we age, we lose our cognitive skills. However, we may know many people in their 70s and 80s who have a memory as good as a teenager's. Good memory is one of the keys to your success, at work in particular. You will perform better at work, speak well, express yourself in an articulate manner, and be more productive.

4) Read books on how to improve your memory, creativity, mental agility, and intelligence.

Develop a habit of reading for at least 30 minutes a day and at least four days a week. Get books on creativity and thinking from a library or buy books of your own. You can buy a tablet computer or an eBook reader and start building a collection of eBooks. That way you can carry thousands of eBooks anywhere and anytime. You should strive to challenge your brain more often with new information and new learning. Start building a library of physical books at your home as well.

Reading books on creativity, memory improvement, and how to play puzzles will force your brain to think in a different way. Your quality of thinking will be different from an average individual's. People might even approach you for help and guidance.

5) Learn what other people did or do in a conundrum similar to yours.

Pay close attention to what other people did in a similar situation as yours and learn from them. Ask for advice from a person you know. You need to ensure that the other person is an expert in that area or is one of your close confidants. Never take advice from people who are cynical or are blabbermouths.

There is a saying that "a wise person is one who learns from his mistakes, but a wiser person is one who learns from other people's mistakes." So learn from your mistakes and do not repeat the same mistakes again and again. Make sure that you learn a lesson, and next time you come across a similar situation, you will be cognizant of what you need to do. Besides, if you are meticulous in studying the gaffes committed by others in a similar situation, you may prevent yourself from falling into a similar predicament.

6) Immerse yourself in nature.

A few times a year, go to the countryside or on a camping trip. Pay close attention to the flora and fauna during your visit. Plan a visit to a bird sanctuary or watch an animal safari and keenly watch the birds and animals. Ask yourself some refined questions like "Am I seeing or am I looking?" "Am I touching or am I feeling?" "Am I listening or am I hearing?" The idea is to use your right brain for strengthening your imagination and artistic skills.

Intriguing yourself in natural environs will reduce your stress level and give you that feel-good factor. This will have a calming effect on your mind. You will stay more focused and your creativity will be enhanced. We as humans have a natural affinity toward nature, as we are a part of nature. We would prefer looking at flowers and trees, mountains and rivers rather than buildings made of concrete and steel. The best time to enjoy nature is during the spring and fall seasons.

7) As adults, learn some things from children.

Spend time with small children and act like a child yourself when you are with them. Tell stories and play indoor and outdoor games with them. The more you engage with kids, the better you will understand the benefits of being childlike.

Watching small kids during playtime can help you enhance your thinking and creativity. Young children do not worry too much; there is no word like *fear* in their dictionary. Sometimes a solution to a problem might come either by talking about it to smart kids or just by observing them while they are playing or talking to each other. Small kids are less judgmental, and they do not stay mad at anybody for too long. Besides, they are carefree, energetic, and happy most of the time. Being happy releases happy hormones called endorphins into our bloodstream, and that has a direct bearing on our creative minds.

8) Learn at least three new words every day.

Use a dictionary or a thesaurus and learn at least three new words every day. At the end of the year, your vocabulary will increase by at least 1,000 new words. Nowadays, you can carry an entire dictionary and thesaurus on a smartphone to use anytime. Some of the dictionary apps also have features like flash cards, bookmarks, word of the day, etc. These features will help you in mastering the words and recalling them at any time. Look out for new words in newspapers and magazines. In short, have a voracious appetite for learning new words.

A strong vocabulary improves and expands your thinking. You can express yourself better while speaking, and you can also express your thoughts and emotions in an unequivocal manner through writing.

9) Learn a foreign language.

Learn a new language through online language courses, audio programs, desktop language-learning software, and books on languages. I like the products offered by Duolingo, Rosetta Stone, and Pimsleur. You may request a native speaker to teach you a foreign language. If that person is interested in your first language, then he can learn it from you as well. It makes a win-win situation for both of you.

Knowing more than one language will give you a competitive edge at work and play. We are living in a world of globalization. The need of the hour is to be multilingual if we want to achieve massive success in life and business. For example, in Europe most people speak more than one language. Learning more than one language will also improve your intellectual skills, bring you more success, and open a plethora of opportunities for you.

10) If you have been doing routine tasks in a certain way, try different methods.

You may have noticed that you have been doing some tasks the same way for years and years. For example, if you have been brushing your teeth with your right hand, try to brush your teeth using your left hand once in a while. If you take the same route to work or school, try a different route the next time. In case you eat only certain types of food, try different ethnic foods. Suppose you read only nonfiction books; try a few fiction books the next time.

If you change the way you do some of your routine tasks every day, you will develop new neural pathways in your brain. It will increase your inquisitiveness and reduce boredom. You will also train your nondominant limbs in doing some of your daily chores.

11) Increase your curiosity and inspiration.

Ask yourself smart questions and try to find the answers. Approach people whom you think are experts in the areas of your interest. Never feel embarrassed about asking for information and solutions. Some people do not read much, but they ask smart questions to the subject matter experts and people wonder how they are so knowledgeable.

If you have extreme inquisitiveness about things around you, it will force your brain to look for solutions to various problems. This will result in dramatic improvement in your knowledge that you can apply in your daily life. This habit will keep your brain healthy in your old age and minimize the chances of getting any neuro-degenerative disorders.

12) Be enthusiastic and excited about life.

We can exude enthusiasm about our life by having a progressive outlook. Accept the reality that life is not always fair to us. We can still try to feel enthusiastic about ourselves, even if we are facing some hardships. When facing an adversity, we should remind ourselves that it is just a transitory phase and the matter will be all right in the end.

Being enthusiastic and optimistic is essential for maintaining high levels of energy. It also increases our ability in problem solving and decision making.

13) Increase your focus and attention span through meditation.

Do some deep-breathing exercises for five to ten minutes a day. Sit on a yoga mat with your legs crossed and focus on your breathing while forgetting about other thoughts, distractions, and noises. You may also maintain a relaxation journal and jot down activities that make you experience total equanimity.

Meditation relaxes our body and mind. Once we are in a deeply relaxed state of mind, we will feel happier, calmer, and rejuvenated.

14) Develop an innate quality of deciphering things that are not obvious the first time.

If you are in a precarious situation, ask yourself the question, "Am I missing something or am I seeing something that is not obvious to me in the first place?" In other words, ask, "Can I discover a meaning that is implied rather than stated in an explicit manner?"

This process will help you go into deep thought about a problem or a situation. In real life, we sometimes overlook something that is quite obvious. Sometimes we are so blind that we cannot see or mull over other possibilities.

15) Listen to music or watch a funny movie to enhance your creativity.

When you go out for a walk or a run, you can take your iPod with you and listen to some soothing music. Music helps to enhance our creativity and makes us feel inspired. You can listen to some soothing music just before you go to bed, as well. There are people who prefer listening to soothing music rather than watching television while eating dinner.

Music brings down our brain wave frequency to put us into a relaxed state of mind. Music lowers the number of thoughts in our brain during those moments. When we have fewer thoughts in our mind, we can think better and more clearly.

16) Become a global thinker to gain a competitive edge.

Stay well informed about what is happening across the globe. For example, keep learning about global economy, politics, significant global events, business opportunities, countries, and people. You may get this information through the Internet, print media, social media, TV, social gatherings, etc. Develop an interest in acquiring these skills.

If you are a global thinker, you will gain a competitive edge over others in career opportunities and general knowledge. You could talk about global trends and current affairs with your colleagues, at social gatherings, and even with your family. This will make your kids knowledgeable as well. You should develop these traits in them while they are growing up.

17) Travel to a foreign country.

Never miss an opportunity to travel to a foreign country. Look for travel deals and book your vacation in advance. To cut down on expenses you could stay in youth hostels, get last-minute bargains, travel with minimum luggage, etc. Some people even visit countries where they have close friends and relatives so they can spend some time with them. Make sure you go through the travel advisories issued by **travel.state.gov** to ensure safe travel. You should also read some good travel books on the countries you are visiting to get firsthand knowledge of those places.

Travel makes you a better person and a more-aware global citizen. It broadens your thinking and your vision. You look at a problem with a different angle and perspective. If you are a business owner, traveling will help you explore new markets for your products and services. Traveling to a foreign country is one of the best ways to reinvigorate yourself and explore different cultures. If possible, start traveling around the globe at a young age and take your entire family with you. When kids start exploring the world, they not only have fun, but they expand their perspective.

18) Study optical illusions.

There are many books available on optical illusions. You can also watch videos on the Internet about optical illusions. Just Google "optical illusion" and you will find a plethora of information.

Optical illusions give you an idea about how different people can identify objects in a picture in different ways. One person sees a rabbit while another person sees a bird in the same picture. Some people will see both of them. Those persons have a keen sense of observation and judgment.

19) Play outdoor sports in which you have to run or stretch your body.

An aging body should not be an excuse for stopping outdoor sports and stretching exercises. On some occasions, you should play games like soccer, tennis, basketball, or baseball. However, when you cross into your 70s, you will need to take it easy on the strenuous cardio activities. After reaching your 70s, spend some time taking long, brisk walks, slow jogging, or some other sports that require limited cardio activity.

Playing outdoor sports brightens your mood, keeps your brain alert, and makes you feel energetic. It is also one of the best methods for curing mild depression and anxiety. Some people stop playing sports or spending quality time outdoors as they get older. Be sure to continue these activities for the sake of your health.

20) Visit an ocean beach for boosting your creativity.

When you get the chance, visit a beach. You can do many creative and calming activities while you are at the ocean. Walk barefoot on the sand for some time. You can walk on the dry sand or get close to the ocean waters on the wet sand. Lie down on the sand, using a beach towel. You can swim and even surf on the ocean waters. You can sit on an easy chair and watch the ocean waves or close your eyes and listen to the waves.

Imagine the sensation deep inside you when you hear the great roars of the waves, and when the ocean breeze dishevels your hair. Simply listening to the waves hitting hard on the shore reduces your stress and makes you feel at peace. The experience is somewhat similar to going into a deep meditative state. This will translate in enhanced peace of mind and happiness. It also makes you more alert and creative. There is scientific evidence that the minerals found in the salty water of the ocean preserve the melatonin, tryptamine, and serotonin levels of our brain. This helps ward off depression and improves our health. The sounds of the ocean wave pattern also decrease our brain frequency to make us feel much calmer.

21) Visit museums and art galleries.

When you are visiting a major city, never miss an opportunity to visit the museums and art galleries. Keep yourself updated about the major attractions in a city. Sometimes you might get a free pass or you can buy cheap tickets over the Internet or at discount-ticket booths.

Whenever you see a priceless artifact in a museum or visit an art gallery, start ruminating deeply about it. You will feel as if you are going back in time, and will wonder how people in the old days used to live and work. Your brain starts thinking deeper and deeper about it and you probably feel inspired and appreciative.

In closing, I am adding a small note to this chapter:

Ask the four "W's and the H" questions as a routine habit: where, when, who, why, and how? I like the "how" questions the most.

Treat your major life decisions as though you are a project manager. A project manager has to look into all the pros and cons of a project, like scope management, risk management, cost management, quality management, change management, etc. You will be delighted to know how much you will lessen your mistakes and bloopers just by thinking like a project manager.

Chapter Two: Health and Wellness

"Age is an issue of mind over matter. If you don't mind, it doesn't matter."
–Mark Twain

Health is wealth. We have been hearing this old saying since we were small kids. The truth is that health is everything. An eighty-year-old person with sound health will enjoy his life more than a forty-year-old person with poor health. That is why it is important to give high priority to your health throughout your lifetime. In fact, we should strive for a health span equivalent to our life span. This means staying in good health during our entire lifetime. If we neglect our health when we are young, it could have far-reaching implications. There is the possibility that when we get old, we will spend our hard-earned money on medication, doctors' visits, procedures, surgeries and hospitalizations.

If you are still not convinced, here is another viewpoint—a short story. Tom, who is 73, has had an amazing family and average health. One day he suffered a major stroke at home that paralyzed one side of his body. He was taken to the nearest hospital. Doctors discovered very high blood cholesterol levels, which had resulted in massive plaque built up in his arteries. This in turn resulted in a blood clot traveling all the way to his brain and causing a massive stroke. The doctors said recovery time would be long and difficult, and Tom would not have the same motor skills that he had had earlier. He had to make several visits to a stroke rehabilitation center for post-hospitalization care.

Now let us talk about the present. Tom has to take several medicines for the rest of his life. His wife and children have to provide extended home care for him, and nobody knows for how long. Sometimes they have to take time off from work. Thus, Tom's illness has affected the whole family. If Tom had undergone regular physical exams in the past and followed his doctor's advice, his situation probably would have been different.

If we are proactive toward our health in our younger days, we can prevent a lot of diseases and hospitalizations in the second half of our lives. However, sometimes episodes do happen, and there are instances where people who are fitness freaks and take good care of their bodies still get sick suddenly. But that percentage is low. Regular exercise, watching what you eat, getting timely physical exams, and sleeping well are some of the things you can do to stay healthy. In fact, doing this may minimize getting significant health issues as you get older.

Here is another story:

Grab a pen in your hand and stretch your arm out all the way in front of you. How long can you hold the pen? I know it sounds a little outlandish, but here is the point: the absolute weight of the pen does not matter. It depends on how long you can keep your arm still while holding the pen. If you hold the pen with your arm outstretched for a minute or so, it will not be a problem. Hold it for an hour or so and your arm will ache. If you hold it for several hours, your arm will feel numb. The longer you stay in this position, the harder it will be to hold the pen. Your arm and hand will feel as if you are holding a ton of weight. The same analogy can be applied to the stresses and worries in life. If you worry about problems for only a little while, nothing happens. Keep thinking about your problems a little longer and they will begin to hurt you. Moreover, if you ruminate about your problems all day long, you will feel paralyzed and incompetent of doing anything.

So always remember to let go of your stress. Do not carry your stress all day long and into the night. Always carrying your stress with you can negatively affect your quality of sleep. Have you heard about the cause-and-effect theory? The stress and its associated symptoms are the effect, but the cause lies somewhere else. So analyze the cause of the problem and it will most likely have a favorable outcome, which is the effect.

All right, now it is time for some health tips. But remember, in case of a life-threatening emergency, always get medical help as soon as possible.

1) Stand tall, sit tall.

When you walk, make sure to stretch your body. Your shoulders should be back, and your head should be up. When you sit, keep your back erect and do not slouch. Avoid using the backrest of the chair when you can.

You will immediately feel a boost in energy. It is one of the best ways to cure anxiety and lack of energy. If you do this consistently throughout your life, you will experience less muscle atrophy and your bones will not shrink dramatically as you age. It is also a good method to improve your level of confidence.

2) Don't sit or stand for too long.

If you have a desk job, put a reminder on your mobile phone to get up every two hours. Alternatively, if you use Microsoft Outlook, set up a two-hour alert reminding you to get up and stretch. You can also take a few steps around the hallway and come back to work after a couple of minutes. Drink water periodically to give you the urge to go to the restroom.

By doing this, you prevent problems to the sciatic nerve that could arise from prolonged sitting, thus avoiding pain in your butt as you get older. You will also reduce eyestrain due to prolonged computer use. New studies have made a convincing case that too much sitting can shorten your life. You can also prevent varicose veins by not standing for extending periods of time. Avoid standing up for more than three to four hours at a time.

3) Undergo regular physical exams every year.

Talk to your doctor about this and keep track of your health results, preferably in digital format, so you can access the reports any time you want. Those of you who love to travel can get a comprehensive body exam done overseas at a fraction of the cost, especially in Asia.

Regular physical exams can prevent many ailments, as you can proactively avoid or detect them before it is too late. They will not rule out all the major illnesses, but they will minimize many major health issues. So make sure to always get your physical exams on time every time.

4) Pay close attention to what you eat.

Before you eat anything, quickly ask yourself whether that food item is good for your health. Is it going to nourish your body and give you energy? I am not saying that you have to start eating organic food from now on, but you should be aware of the pros and cons of the food you eat. Avoid junk food, too much sugar, French fries, high-fructose corn syrup, processed foods, candies, soda, energy drinks, and fatty foods. Instead of these unhealthy foods, switch to alkaline foods like vegetables and fruits, soups and salads, foods high in fiber, lean meats, etc.

When you become aware of the nutritional benefits or the overall health risks associated with a particular food item, you will be more mindful of what you eat. You will probably minimize eating foods that are low in nutritional value even though they may have a great taste. You will notice a slow transformation within your body, and you will feel more energetic and alert.

5) Visualize yourself being healthy, enthusiastic, and energetic just before you fall asleep.

Before you fall asleep at night, gently close your eyes and start imagining a healthy, energetic, peaceful, and enthusiastic you for around ten minutes. Perceive those sensations and vibrations in your body. Repeat the same activity for around ten minutes every morning while lying in bed, then get up and start your day.

The power of your subconscious mind works for you the entire night while you are sleeping, as well as during the day while you are awake. Think of this long enough and your subconscious mind will produce healthy thought patterns and habits for you automatically. If you do this religiously every day, you will start feeling energetic and positive all the time.

6) If something has been mentally or emotionally perturbing you for a long time, address that matter as soon as you can.

Do some self-talk in a quiet place and ruminate over your problem. Try to first find a solution yourself based on your experience. If that does not help, talk to a trusted friend or an advisor. Immensely engage in your job during the day or some creative activity so that you get a little time to ponder over your negative emotions. As a last alternative, get help from a trusted doctor.

A leading cause of short-term or long-term depression and mood swings is thinking about issues and problems repeatedly for a long time almost every day and night. This behavior changes the chemical composition of our brain, which results in some devastating effects on our mental and emotional well-being. If there is no solution to your problem, try to overlook it completely. Remind yourself that thinking about it continually will undermine your brain's functionality. When confronted in life with a situation we have no control over, we should challenge ourselves to change.

7) Carry out various tasks 15 to 20 percent faster than your normal speed.

Walk and run a little faster than you usually do. Exercise a little faster. At work, deliver your projects a little more quickly, but meticulously. Type a little faster on your computer, for example, when composing an email. Talk a little faster and gesture while talking.

When you do various activities a little more quickly, you increase your energy level. You are more alert and active. Your brain starts thinking faster and processes information faster. With speed, you can accomplish more in less time. If you develop a habit of doing various tasks faster at a young age, in your old age you will continue to do things faster than others will.

8) If you have a sedentary job, move your legs and arms every 15 to 20 minutes and do stretching exercise every few hours.

Periodically exercise your legs while sitting on a chair. For example, raise your toes while keeping your sole on the ground, hold for a few seconds and then move your toes back to the ground. Repeat this ten times. Next, keep your toes firmly on the ground, raise your soles all the way up, hold for a few seconds and bring your soles back to the ground. Repeat these stretches every few hours. You can also go for a quick walk during lunchtime.

Doing these exercises will improve the blood circulation in your legs as well as strengthen your calves and the veins in your legs.

9) Lower the number of thoughts you get in your brain every day.

According to National Science Foundation we get between 12,000 to 50,000 thoughts per day at the conscious and the subconscious level, depending upon how deeply one thinks. We need to bring that number down, and meditation can help us do that. With meditation, we bring more self-awareness to ourselves. It calms our nerves and we are able to sleep better. There are many other ways to reduce our recurring thoughts too, such as exercising, traveling, social engagement, listening to soothing music, etc.

It is the quality of our thoughts that matters, not the quantity. In fact, there is a direct correlation between our thinking and our overall health. When we keep thinking too much, we are essentially tiring our brain and losing our focus and creativity.

10) Drink at least eight to twelve 8-ounce glasses of water a day.

You should consume at least 2 to 3 liters of water a day. Men need more water than women do. After getting up early in the morning and brushing your teeth, drink two glasses of water. This helps flush toxins out of the body. You should also drink water 30 minutes before your lunch or dinner and consume several additional glasses of water during the day. Consume tea and coffee moderately and stop drinking soda. Studies have linked regular soda and diet soda consumption to increased risks of obesity, damaged teeth, elevated blood pressure, kidney disease and so on.

Your brain will work more efficiently if you keep your body hydrated. When you ingest a glass of water every few hours, you are flushing toxins from your digestive track. Without water, the contents of your colon can dry out and eventually cause constipation. Some other benefits of drinking water include helping with weight loss, healthier-looking skin, healthier kidneys, strengthened muscles, and carrying nutrients to our cells. Some people do not like drinking water at all. However, the benefits of drinking water far outweigh the dislike toward its tastelessness.

11) Socialize with friends and family for longevity.

Take your family on vacations occasionally. Make new friends and hang out with energetic and happy people. Organize block parties in your neighborhood, participate in potlucks with friends, and take part in sports.

We humans cannot live in isolation. There is scientific evidence that people who are more outgoing and social live longer and do not get sick often, especially in old age. This is a wake-up call for people who like solitude.

12) Eat breakfast to improve your heart's health, boost metabolism, and get a good start to the day.

Even if you do not like eating breakfast in the morning, start with something small like a banana or a few scoops of yogurt. Once it becomes a habit every morning, start adding more items to your breakfast. Keep reminding yourself that a healthy breakfast has huge health benefits. Gradually a new habit will form.

Your metabolism is at its peak in the morning. You need more energy in the morning to start your day. Besides, eating a healthy breakfast will keep you energetic in the first few hours of the day. Eating breakfast will also help you with weight control and heart health.

13) Challenge your brain every day to improve your brain function.

Develop an interest in puzzles, crosswords, problem solving, mathematical calculations, and so on. At first it will be hard to cultivate this new habit. However, if you persevere and take an active interest, things will start getting better. Gradually you will notice a subtle change in your brainpower as you are pushing your brain to think.

If you use your brain in challenging activities, you will develop new neural connections in your brain and improve your cognitive skills. This means you will have a strong memory, even in your old age. You will feel sharper and more alert, and that should build a strong motivation to continue doing it.

14) Add turmeric to your diet.

Mix a pinch of turmeric powder into your soup or salad. You can also add a pinch of turmeric to a glass of milk. Add a teaspoon of honey for a better taste.

Turmeric has cancer-fighting power and anti-inflammatory benefits too. It increases your bone density and is good for your skin.

15) If you already have a serious illness, show tenacity and visualize your body healing at the cellular level.

Remind yourself often, and with assertiveness, that you are healing and getting better. It might sound paradoxical to you initially, but do it anyway. Perceive those emotions of exuberance of a lively and healthy body several times throughout the day and night. In essence, you are daydreaming about a healthy body and a healthy you instead of feeling sorry about your illness. Talk to people who have overcome a similar illness and draw encouragement from them. Laugh as much as you can; this helps boost the immune system. Laughter also helps in pain management and reducing stress levels. Read inspirational books and books on your illness. You also need to develop strong mental, emotional, and spiritual energies. There are physically healthy people out there who are unhappier than some people who are suffering from several physical ailments. They reason that they are not strong mentally, emotionally, and spiritually.

When some people learn that they have a serious illness or must follow a lengthy treatment plan, they become melancholy and feel hopeless. However, during those moments, if you become strong mentally, emotionally, and spiritually and have a firm belief that you will overcome this tough time, miracles can happen. By reaffirming your faith and by staying extremely positive, you are reprogramming your subconscious mind to help you in the healing process.

16) Visit your dentist regularly to keep your teeth healthy.

Visit your dentist regularly for checkups and preventive care. Brush twice a day and floss your teeth every day.

Clean, white teeth give a beautiful smile, so strive for healthy teeth and healthy gums. The health of your teeth has a direct bearing on the health of your heart. According to the American Academy of Periodontology, people with periodontal disease are almost twice as likely to have heart disease.

17) Exercise for at least 45 minutes a day.

At least three or four days a week, run for 20 minutes early in the morning. If you do not like to run, you may walk briskly for 30 minutes. Next, do some stretching exercises or yoga for 20 minutes. Alternatively, you can join a gym and work with a fitness trainer.

Exercising regularly will keep your heart fit and your brain alert. It will also improve your mood and energy level. People who are suffering from minor depression will benefit a lot by taking brisk walks, running, doing yoga, and doing muscle-building exercises.

18) Be an early riser and wake up between 4:00 AM and 5:00 AM.

If you have a problem getting up early in the morning, set an alarm clock. Let the alarm go off 15 minutes earlier than your usual wake-up time. Do not use the snooze button on the alarm clock; just get up right away. Open some windows to let in some fresh morning air or step out of your home and breathe in some fresh air. After that, come back and start your daily routine. After about a week, try to get up an additional 15 minutes earlier. Keep repeating this process until you start getting up between 4:00 AM and 5:00 AM, depending on what time you go to sleep. Now spend this extra time in going out for a run, taking a shower, practicing meditation, eating breakfast, and doing some office work.

People who rise early have better health and energy, and are more successful at work than late risers. In fact, people who rise early and go to sleep early live longer and are happier than people who wake up late. There are no distractions during morning hours and waking up early can give you an hour or two of extra time for focus and creativity.

19) Take two-minute deep breaths several times a day.

Whether you are sitting, standing, or lying down on a bed, take several deep breaths for a few minutes. Breathe in up to a count of four and hold your breath up to a count of ten. Then release your breath through your mouth up to a count of eight.

Our brain makes up only 2% of our body mass, but it needs 30% of oxygen. If we are anxious or worried, we normally breathe shallowly. However, if we feel relaxed, we breathe more naturally. By taking deep breaths several times a day, we are giving more oxygen to the brain. This keeps our brain alert and agile. Besides, deep breathing also helps reduce our stress levels and makes us feel more tranquil. Some of the indications of stress are fast breathing, increased heart rate, and high blood pressure. Deep breathing can help regulate these symptoms.

20) Perform neck exercises every day, especially if you hunch over your computer all day.

Start with simple and gentle neck stretching exercises. Turn your head slowly toward your right shoulder and then turn back to the normal position. Now turn your head toward your left shoulder and return to the normal position. Next tilt your head all the way forward so your chin touches your chest; feel the stretch for a few seconds and come back to the normal position. Then tilt your head all the way back and feel the stretch in your neck. After a few seconds, you can come back to your usual position.

Doing neck exercises helps strengthen the muscles of the neck, upper back, and shoulders. It makes the neck more flexible, and if you include the shoulder exercises with it, then you will not slouch too much during old age. Besides, if you have strong neck muscles, your brain will receive a good blood supply. Neck pain can cause other symptoms, such as weakness and numbness in the arms and legs. Weak neck muscles can also create problems in balance or coordination and can impair motor skills.

21) Schedule walking meetings occasionally, as long as no more than four people participate.

Instead of the conventional method of organizing meetings in a conference room, try walking meetings. You and your team can take a long walk, and all of you can simultaneously engage in a meeting. However, this technique will not work if your team has to give a presentation or if your office is located in a busy metropolitan area.

One of the biggest benefits of these walking meetings is that your body can get some exercise. You are also breathing fresh air, and if the environment around your workplace is picturesque, more creativity will flow in your brain. You never know when that great idea might come into your mind. Just ensure that the weather is congenial for these meetings. An early-morning time would be ideal for walking meetings.

22) Have a belly laugh a few times a day.

Associate with people who have a good sense of humor. Occasionally watch a funny movie with your family or friends, and read some great joke books. Laugh at your silly mistakes or laugh for no reason at all without feeling the need to explain yourself.

Having a belly laugh has many health benefits. It triggers the release of endorphins, which are the body's natural painkillers. It is a great cardio workout, especially for people who are frail and weak and who cannot do any vigorous workouts. Another major benefit of a great belly laugh is that it can tone your abdominal muscles. So make sure that you have a belly laugh a few times every day.

I want to end this chapter with a strong emphasis on one word—and that word is **happy.**

Be happy: Yes, I know it is not always easy to do—but let us try an exercise that may offer you a paradigm of sorts:

Think about a situation when you were very sad, stressed, and feeling dejected. Perceive that emotion deeply as if you are in that state of mind right now. What happens to your body? Are you feeling energetic? Check to see if you are slouching, with your shoulders angled forward.

With this one exercise, you have just succeeded in making yourself feel terrible. No worries; I will not leave you there.

Now reach back into your past and consider a situation when you were at your best. Think about one of the proudest moments of your life—an achievement that left you proud to be you. Think of that event, place, or thing that left an indelible imprint in your mind. How does it feel? Now check your posture. A bit more energetic? Feeling positive? Are your shoulders moved back and is your head straight?

Perfect happiness is elusive. But if you begin a journey that requires you to "behave as if" you are happy even if you do not experience it, in the long run you will benefit from simply trying. Happiness is a goal to be achieved whenever possible, which means being happy is a choice. Oh, and by the way—it is free!

Chapter Three: Career Success

"It is better to be a failure at something you love than to be a success at something you hate."
–George Burns

If you have had progressive career growth so far, then congratulations to you. You should be proud of your achievements and your contributions to all the companies you have worked with. Keep doing a great job and follow your passion.

However, if you had some past career setbacks, do not become despondent. After all, they were temporary career stumbling blocks. Your past career failures should not have any bearing on your forthcoming career path. Likewise, in case you face setbacks in your career in the future, that too shouldn't be inimical to your self-confidence or your potential. You can turn around your professional life if you believe in yourself and your capabilities, along with showing perseverance. Do not worry about what people might think as far as you are concerned or evaluate their reactions.

Here is one solid piece of advice about having an incredible career: Do more of what you extremely love to do and a somewhat reasonable amount of something you do not like all that much. Do very little of what you do not like to do at all. You do not have to please anybody, not even your family or your friends, by considering their conflicting opinions about your career. This holds more credence when you have just started in your career. The only exception is if they know you well or if they are experts in your field. If you go by what other people tell you in career matters just to please them, it could have unwanted ramifications on your career graph. In the end, that phenomenal success that you have been longing for will evade you for a while. In other words, it will take you longer to achieve an incredible success in your career if you are doing it to please others, not yourself.

Sometimes due to financial constraints or a bad economy, some people have to take any type of job to earn a living, even if their passion lies somewhere else. Nevertheless, my advice to them would be to keep looking out for their true self and find opportunities in an industry they love. In due course, just quit your current job and follow your dreams.

I have seen people changing careers in their mid-forties and fifties, after working in their previous industry for decades and decades. I have seen how happy they are now. They have achieved real success in life, even though it was during the second half of their lives. Their output has increased in a dramatic way. They are happy, healthy, and sleeping better.

Let us start with the career tips. These tips will be helpful for experienced executives, as well as individuals who have recently joined the workforce. Even college and university students will find the information outlined below helpful.

1) Think about your career goals at a very young age, and keep brainstorming about them.

Keep a journal about your hobbies along with all of your likes and dislikes. When you document your likes and dislikes for a long time, some activities will have many repetitions in the journal. This is where you will find your mojo. Get career counseling from experts in those areas, as well as advice from your parents and friends.

When you are aware of your career ambitions at a young age, your professional life starts shaping in that direction, although you may face some impediments at first. Eventually you will start realizing what you are truly good at and what you do best. Then, all you have to do is find the right work and the right company to show your competence.

2) Perform extremely well during your formative years in school and college and later reap the rewards for life.

If you perform well in your middle and high school, you will have better chances of being admitted into a great college. The likelihood of getting a scholarship increase many-fold. In certain family situations, if you have to get an educational loan, do not hesitate about it. However, you still need to do your research and select the best choice.

If you have completed your formal education with a bachelor's degree and possibly a master's degree with a high GPA, you stand a much better chance of landing your first job with a great company. So invest heavily in education.

3) Land your first job with a big company.

Identify some companies where you would love to work. Do intensive research on those companies. Talk to people who work there, or talk to former employees of those companies. Once you complete your formal education, try every source and every way to get a foot in the door of one of these big companies. You may also take the help of your professional network, college alumni, social media, friends, staffing firms, and so on.

If you get your first job in a big company—say, a publicly listed company—you will have a better chance of landing your next job with another good company. The reason is that you already will have worked for a well-known company in the past. Besides, a well-known company will give you a better starting salary and other company benefits. However, if you start your first job with a small company, then it could probably take you a little longer to find your next job. Once you have worked for a large company for a while, you can switch to a smaller company—say, a startup—or work for another large company.

4) Adapt your working style to your boss's.

When you start a new job, have frequent meetings with your boss and ask specific questions about his working style. You may also watch his body language to get some clues. Observe whether your boss is authoritative or whether he believes in a consensus in decision making. Notice whether he is more visual (prefers updates in writing), auditory (likes to get updates while talking), or kinesthetic (uses all the senses, is emotional, and looks at the big picture).

If you mirror your boss's working style, you will develop more synergy and a strong working relationship. This will translate into more success and growth in your current position.

5) Keep your boss happy and your boss's boss happier.

Have a one-on-one meeting with your boss's boss occasionally. Tell him about the assignments you are handling, and any challenges that you are facing. Ask if you could be of any help to him. Keep your boss informed about the agenda of such meetings.

If your boss's boss is happy with your work, it means he thinks that his direct report (who is your boss) is doing a great job. It might create opportunities for your boss's promotion. Eventually that might lead to a promotion for you as well. However, you have to prove your value to the company. If you are doing a phenomenal job, then your chances for a promotion are fair.

6) Show up 15 minutes earlier and leave 15 minutes later than other people at work.

Give enough time to yourself to maneuver morning rush hour so you can reach your office 15 minutes early. There could be traffic, an accident, or other obstacles on your way to work.

Getting to the office 15 minutes earlier than most people will give you time to settle down. You can have a brief chat with your peers and co-workers. You will also get a few moments to set priorities for your day. In addition, you should plan the day's agenda the previous night so you are prepared for your day.

7) Maintain harmonious relationships with your peers.

Collaborate on various projects and show true professionalism. Try to develop synergy and a win-win situation for everybody. If you have to deal with a difficult person at work on a daily basis, schedule a one-on-one meeting with that person and express your concerns. Make him aware that his attitude and approach are going to be damaging to the department's functioning. In addition, assure him that you are going to listen to him and consider his viewpoints on the business problem. You need to incorporate the best possible solution to a problem, and remember that it is all right to disagree in a professional manner.

If you have good professional relationships with your peers, it will improve your productivity, reduce work-related stress, and keep you motivated and energetic.

8) Check and respond to your emails only a few times each day; you do not need to respond immediately after they have arrived in your inbox.

Instead of reading emails from multiple devices as they arrive, schedule specific email times when you can be at your computer, usually only a few times each day. The rest of the time you should be working on projects. Scan your emails in the morning and flag emails that require immediate attention. You may also set up rules within your email program so that important emails move automatically into a VIP folder. That way, you will respond to the senders of the VIP emails on a priority basis, although only once or twice a day. After checking your email in the morning, you should check again at around 2:00 PM and mentally start planning how to respond. After this, go back to work again. Then around 4:00 PM, start composing your responses and sending emails.

If you read and respond to emails the moment they arrive, it will distract your mind, and you will not be able to give undivided attention to your job. You will be delaying your projects, and tasks will start piling up at your desk.

9) Treat your direct reports with respect and make them your allies.

Make sure that you listen to your subordinates, inspire them so they perform well at work. Reinforce working harder and smarter for their department and their own selves.

Some bosses try to show authority through intimidation and micromanagement, thinking that their direct reports will comply out of fear. However, employees thrive and are more productive in a direct, open, and collaborative environment.

10) Choose and commit to a challenging project. If you succeed, it could bring more revenues to your company.

Be the first person to volunteer for a difficult project in your company. Sometimes you may not be an expert in a particular area, and that is fine. If you have great people-management skills, you will find a way to succeed by collaborating with subject-matter experts and your team. If there are no knowledgeable workers in your company, you could hire external consultants on the project.

If you are the person who commits to a difficult project, you will gain respect and recognition in your company. You will become the person who is willing to take risks and make difficult tasks possible. You may not succeed 100% of the time, but your superiors will appreciate that you have at least tried. This is one of the best secrets to growing faster within your company.

11) Don't waste time in office politics and gossipmongering.

Do a great job and be valuable to your company. Be at arm's length with gossipmongers and people who play office politics. You do not have to avoid them; just do not develop a deep friendship. It is okay to exchange pleasantries when you see them. When you work with them on various projects, you should deal with them in a professional manner.

Office politics, nepotism, and rumormongers drain your energy level and waste your precious time. Gossipmongers are not productive at work and they cannot be your best friends and cohorts. When you become part of the gossipmongering group or backstabbers, people will start avoiding you. Rumormongers might even spread rumors and blame you for them. In this process, you lose valuable time, trust, and goodwill.

12) Give all your energy and soul to your work when you enter your office in the morning.

Be in the zone, which means that your actual skills match the perceived performance requirements at work. When you are in a zone, you keep all of your troubles, problems, and issues at bay while you are working. Unless there is a pressing situation demanding urgent attention in your personal life, you are better off focusing on your work.

A distraction-free mind will make you a better employee and you will become more productive. If you leave your personal worries and hitches aside when you enter your office, you can develop razor-sharp focus at work and do an amazing job.

13) Occasionally offer help to people in other business groups or departments, even if the job falls outside your roles and responsibilities.

Assume that you have a chance meeting with a co-worker in a different department and you realize that he cannot solve a chronic business problem. Offer your assistance if you have the expertise in that area. However, you should be sure that your own projects do not suffer because of your generous offer of help.

You will gain recognition by the head of the other business group if you solve their problem. When your manager gets the news, she will realize how indispensable you are for the company.

14) Be the first to break the bad news; your boss will not like last-minute surprises.

Always keep your boss in the loop about problems that you may be facing in your projects. If you do not, then problems can exacerbate and will have far-reaching implications. There is a saying, "A stitch in time saves nine." It is better to feel embarrassed one time rather than face a catastrophe in the end.

If you withhold information about project failures and difficulties faced due to circumstances beyond your control or due to lack of expertise, you are accountable for any consequences. Sometimes, if the stakes are high, it might even cost you your job. It is better to be bold and candid while giving the bad news to your supervisor. You might get support from your boss in taking a corrective action.

15) Always strive to take the initiative.

If you have a burning desire to give exceptional performance at work, you may be a risk taker and initiate tasks or projects before anybody else does.

In fact, you will not make any excuses for the jobs assigned to you either.

As an initiator, you will be considered a self-starter, and motivated people will follow you willingly. This is one of the qualities of a great leader. At the end of the day, you will get more and more responsibilities, which will translate into future career growth.

16) Learn how to work with diverse cultures.

If you work for companies that have a global presence, you will work with people from diverse cultures. You may perhaps travel to international destinations on business, so it will be helpful to know a little bit about other cultures and traditions.

If diverse minds work together on a problem, more solutions are possible. People will think in their own ways for problem solving and decision making. Remember the future of major businesses lies in having a global footprint, which means embracing diversity. So work locally but think globally.

17) Be a voracious reader and aim for continual learning opportunities.

Make it a habit of reading for at least 30 minutes a day. You may read about a subject of your liking or your profession, a self-help book, or any book on personal development. Some people do not like reading. I would recommend audio books for those people, and listening to them especially in the car or during morning workouts.

If you commit to lifelong learning, you will perform better at work and home. You will have a competitive edge over your peers. Besides, you will know how other people respond to particular problems by studying them and taking action. There is a saying, "A wise person is one who learns from his mistakes, but a wiser person is one who learns from other people's mistakes." Biographies and autobiographies are a great help in getting a perspective about a problem.

18) Be a credit giver, not a credit taker.

Praise people who do a great job, even though you might have contributed to the project. This is especially effective when you praise people in front of others for a job well done. This small act motivates people to perform even better. Besides, you get praise in return for your magnanimity.

If you take credit for a job done by other people, it might look good to your boss at first. However, facts speak for themselves. You will make fewer friends in the end.

19) During the first month at your new job, get to know all key people within your company.

Browse the company intranet (if you have one) or the employee directory to learn about key people with whom you may or may not interface on a regular basis. Schedule a one-on-one meeting with them to introduce yourself and to learn about them.

Knowing important people within your company will help you perform your job better and faster. You will know ahead of time whom to approach when a particular business problem is to be addressed.

20) Schedule monthly team lunches and frequent one-on-ones with your direct reports.

Send a lunch invitation to your team from time to time. This will help you make a strong connection with your direct reports outside of work. During the lunch, all of you should talk about your interests and hobbies, about your likes, dislikes, and so on. You could also organize some sports events and ensure active participation of everybody.

If a team takes part in extracurricular activities, it helps the team build rapport and participate in social engagements. The employees perform better at work. They do not see each other as competitors, but as individuals who are working collectively and mobilizing one other for common aspirations.

21) Master the important technology needed for your job.

Develop an inquisitive mind in picking up the essential technology skills at work. If some concepts are hard, start learning them at your own pace through books, web-based training, instructor-led training, CDs, DVDs, MP3, etc.

If you master the relevant technology to perform your job, you will do things faster, more efficiently, and with fewer errors. You will notice that as you get the knack of basic technical skills and embrace new and changing technology, your work will become easier and more enjoyable.

22) Be a leader, a follower and a collaborator.

Sometimes, you should lead people to accomplish a mission. Other times you should follow or team up with people who are experts on a particular subject.

Being a leader will help you to become a role model for other people, and you will become the person they want to look up to. At other times, people will realize that you are a humble person who is willing to follow others. This is irrespective of the position you hold within your company.

23) Improve your writing skills.

The best way to improve your business writing skills is to write on a regular basis. Take an online course in how to write better or read books on writing well.

If you are an effective writer, it will help you communicate better in writing with your co-workers. An ineffective written communication may cause others to misinterpret your message.

24) Stay well informed in your industry.

Talk to experts in your industry or develop new connections. Have frequent conversations with your friends and exchange information about your areas of interest. There are many magazines, blogs, and websites that can keep you updated in your field.

Know about future trends in your industry to help you plan and manage your career according to changing times. You should also acquire some skillsets relevant to the dynamics of emerging markets. This approach will give you a competitive edge as well.

25) When you start your career, work very hard in the first and second decades (in your 20s and 30s).

Work longer hours, work smarter, work in an effective manner, manage your time well, and plan your days ahead of time. You should follow these principles thoroughly in your 20s and 30s.

Achieve as much as you can in your career in as little time as possible. When you are in your 50s and 60s, you will not be able to put in very long hours at work due to age and lower energy levels. You will reap the benefits of hard work done in your early career days in your elder years.

26) Handle one big project at a time and give it your best.

Prioritize your work, and first complete the projects that are most important and yield high returns. Work one project at a time.

When you give undivided attention to a large project, the quality of work is impeccable. However, if you work on multiple major projects at the same time, there is the possibility that you may lose some traction by switching between projects. Sometimes there are exceptions, and you may be working on multiple projects because of a business requirement. In that case, do the best you can.

27) Improve your typing speed.

As we mostly type on computers, tablets, and smartphones now, we should learn how to type faster. Some people prefer to use only a few fingers, but if you learn to use all fingers on a keyboard, your typing speed will increase in a considerable manner. You may also try some speech-to-text software products, like Dragon Naturally Speaking. In fact, you can create documents three times faster than typing by hand and with 99% accuracy.

If you increase your typing speed, you can create documents, spreadsheets, memos, emails, presentations, etc., in less time, thereby freeing some of your time that you can use in other activities.

28) Improve your voice and diction.

People say singing at a high and low pitch for a few minutes every day makes their voice deeper and more powerful. You may also consider working with a voice coach. There are some great books available on this subject as well, like books authored by Roger Love. In addition, drinking a lot of water helps keep your voice box in top shape.

A commanding voice can be a potent tool in your career success. You will become more assertive. In addition, when you have inflections in your voice, you make a firsthand impression on the minds of others. People will listen to you with rapt attention.

29) Write a book on a subject of your liking.

Nowadays, it is easy to self-publish a book, especially an eBook. You can write an eBook for the Amazon Kindle platform, Apple iBookstore, or Barnes & Noble Nook. You can talk to some literary agents who can probably get you a book deal through a publisher. Your focus should be on creating high-quality content that can add some unique value to the reader.

Apart from your career achievements and job history, how would the hiring manager feel if you mentioned your book to him during a job interview? Besides, book writing is one of the best ways to leave your enduring legacy. Your progeny will know about you through your writings.

30) Know something outside your area of expertise.

Read about current affairs, world politics, the economy, etc. Keep yourself updated about happenings around the globe through TV, print media, and the Internet. You may also exchange information about relevant topics with your family and friends.

Being current and well informed about global happenings will improve your job performance. You will be able to take corrective action according to the market dynamics. Your thinking will improve and you will come up with new ideas and solutions to business problems. Sometimes a solution to a problem might come from knowing or studying material outside your area of know-how.

31) Think about bringing changes to your business processes on a regular basis.

Think about whether or not there are better ways to solve your business problems. You may come up with different scenarios and engage in brainstorming sessions with your team. Take notes, keep journals, use mind-mapping software. If we think in a different way than most people do, we can come up with innovative ideas and unique solutions to solve a problem.

Do not be complacent about methods and processes. Just because certain jobs have been done in a particular way for years and years, that does not mean you have to maintain the status quo. Sometimes there is a better way to perform tasks in less time and with greater efficiency. Look how quickly technology has changed our lives after the advent of the internet.

32) If you lose your job, go into a massive job-hunting mode.

Always keep a current copy of your resume, even if you are working. If you lose your job, it is normal to feel disillusioned for a few days and vent your emotions. However, you need to accept the reality, cheer up, keep a positive mental attitude, and start looking for a new job right away. Contact all of your friends, acquaintances, and past co-workers. Engage in social media in a conscientious manner and find ways to contact hiring managers and decision makers working for companies in your industry.

Be vigilant about company plans for redeployment, extreme cost cutting, and a hiring freeze. These are not good signs and should raise a red flag. Some of the explanations for your job loss could be the company's going out of business or your performance issues. Other reasons could be the company's closing some office locations, cultural fit issues, or your inability to get along well with your boss or peers.

33) If you have performance issues at work, address it on a proactive basis.

Approach your boss and address his concerns about your job performance. Have a healthy and open two-way conversation. Do it much ahead of the annual performance review meeting. Be genuine and assure him that you will show better results the next time. Schedule performance preview meetings with your supervisor every month to monitor your progress.

If you have performance issues and do not address them early, you risk losing your job. Besides, if you have burnout at work, the first thing it will do is take its toll on your health. Perhaps you could be a better fit in a different group or department. On the other hand, you just may not be the right fit for the company. In this case, start looking for a new job.

34) Handle difficult people at work with some objectivity, emotional control, and a little diplomacy.

First, find out why the individual is behaving in a manner that is harmful to the health of the organization. You may need to ask some open-ended questions in a discreet manner and listen to his responses. Show empathy to the difficult person by being nonjudgmental and listening most of the time. It is normal that the person could have an emotional outburst after a while. This action is going to bring good results when it is over. Once the difficult person begins to feel understood, and he feels there is somebody he can trust, he will start displaying behavioral changes.

If you treat difficult people with poise, respect, and diplomacy, you can work together in most situations. If you show similar arrogance and are egoistic, it will be detrimental to the organization's health and sooner or later to your own performance. By the way, there are difficult people in all companies and every organization. Your job should be to minimize the negative impact those people could have on your day-to-day job by working with them on building a rapport.

35) Learn the "Do It Now" habit to eliminate procrastination.

Perhaps you are procrastinating on a specific project because of laziness or because you do not know how to do it. In a case where you do not have expertise on something, you can delegate that job to experts. Besides, if you have to complete a project or a small task even though it is not due for another week or two, why not do it now if time allows? Once you develop this sense of urgency in completing various tasks, you will get more time to work on other activities.

This simple habit will go a long way in dealing with procrastination as you will start and complete your work ahead of schedule. This is true with small errands in particular. If you have to complete minor tasks at work and each of them will only take a few moments, do them now rather than later.

36) If people do a poor job over and over again at work, do not get overly emotional thinking they will feel bad if you talk about it.

If you are trying not to hurt your co-worker by expressing your disappointment about how poorly he carried out a project, then you are doing yourself a great disservice. In fact, you need to speak about it in an assertive manner, while maintaining your poise. Use your people-management skills to address these kinds of situations.

Many people sabotage their careers by trying to be too nice to conceited and insincere people at work. Those types of people take them for granted. Therefore, work on improving your emotional intelligence. There are some good books available on this subject, like some written by Daniel Goleman.

37) Associate yourself with smart and hardworking people.

Identify high-performing teams and individuals in your organization and never miss an opportunity to have face time with them. In essence, you are displaying your visibility to them. If you indeed need to learn from smart people, be part of their coterie. Make yourself available if they need your help and contribute your expertise on their projects.

Working with high-performing individuals will keep you motivated and focused and will increase your levels of energy and enthusiasm. You will always be ready for the next big challenge at work. After all, you will learn a lot from them, and they will learn a lot from you along the way.

38) Take lifelong action in self-improvement.

Always strive to take action in learning new things, improving your image, developing extreme curiosity, having a positive mental attitude, and so on. Be willing to receive constructive feedback from people who care about you.

If you make a firm resolve to engage in lifelong learning and self-improvement, you will face fewer setbacks in life. Your career growth will head in the right direction. You could improve the lives of some people who matter to you the most by sharing the lessons of life learned.

39) Dress upward and get an excellent haircut.

Make sure you wear neat, clean, and ironed clothes according to your job and the dress code. Men should trim their hair every 2 to 3 weeks. Women should also keep a decent hairstyle relevant to their job.

If you dress a little upward, it will make you look more sophisticated and professional. People always like well-groomed individuals at both work and play.

40) Work with a mentor and be a mentor.

You should have a mentor for continuous career success. Engage with a mentor at your workplace or hire a professional coach. You can also try peer coaching. In peer coaching, you select a peer at work and both of you coach each other. You meet once or twice a month for coaching sessions. And guess what? You do not have to pay anything for these peer-coaching meetings.

An experienced mentor will guide you through rough times at work. He can give helpful feedback, suggestions, and motivation and strengthen your confidence. A good mentor will even give you advance warning signs of any major pitfalls at work. However, make sure the mentor you select is competent, inspiring, and honest.

41) Be good at remembering names.

When you meet new people, show marked interest in them. After hearing their names, repeat them internally several times. During the conversation, say their names a few times. With the process of repetition, you will commit their names to memory.

If you are good at remembering names, you will make more friends and people would like to have your company. Imagine having a chance meeting with a person whom you met only once several years back and remembering his name, even though he may not remember yours. He will appreciate your receptive mind.

42) Don't complain or whine.

Just do your job without complaining or making excuses. Every person has some problems, but that should not prevent you from doing your job. Do not be lazy and do not whine. Just do the work with no excuses.

If you find faults in other people or in your job, you will not be able to achieve colossal success at work. You will slow down and your performance will take a hit. This attitude will drain your mental and emotional energies as well.

43) Motivate others.

Give constant encouragement and positive vibes to others. Do not be condescending and do not let people down. Stay away from people who think in a negative way all the time, even though you might have tried your level best to help them.

When we have a positive and enriching work environment, we excel at work and everything suits our tastes and temperaments.

A short note to end this chapter:

If you want to be indispensable to a company or even if you are an entrepreneur, just do great work. Develop a strong obsession to be productive at work. Remember, being busy at work does not always mean that one is productive. Bring revenues to the company and save money for the company. Above all, work with complete honesty and integrity.

Chapter Four: Family and Relationships

"Family is not an important thing; it is everything."
–Michael J. Fox

Have you noticed some couples in a very loving and healthy relationship even after decades of married life? You may also have seen people separating after a short marriage. At times it is unavoidable, but sometimes reconciliation is a possibility. Think about a family where everybody is a role model. We wish we could imitate them and draw inspiration from their actions. In this perfect family, the couple trusts and loves each other unconditionally.

In this family kids are raised in a positive and confident manner. The kids have high self-esteem, and they possess most of the qualities that are necessary to succeed in today's competitive environment. There is no individual or family where every aspect of life is super perfect. However, we may know individuals and families that are almost perfect in most areas of life. So what are the secrets of a healthy and happy married life? In this short nugget, I am going to touch base on a few important relationship concepts.

1) Focus on the positives in your spouse and kids.

Look at the positives in your spouse rather than finding faults, and be less judgmental. You can always give feedback to your spouse or kids on something when you feel some improvement is required. After all, it is in the interest of everybody because you care for them. The same logic applies to you as well. You also have to accept feedback from your spouse—and even from your kids—to be a better husband or wife, father, mother, son, or daughter.

Remember, if you lose your job, your health, your finances, or all of your resources, what is the one thing that will always be by your side? It is your family. Therefore, it is your job to nurture your family in every possible manner. Just overlook trivial bloopers and develop the habit of "forgive and forget." If you want people to change their outlook, you have to go first. Maybe they will be inspired to improve on their own efforts.

2) Trust is the most important element in a relationship.

Be truthful with yourself and your spouse. Do not keep anything hidden from each other. Remember, trust is a two-way process that can flourish only if both the partners are willing to work on it. Showing compassion and deep caring for your partner during tough times also helps strengthen trust.

If there is a lack of trust in a relationship (say, between spouses or kids), then the relationship is going to take a beating. The foundation of any relationship is trust, and you should always find ways to strengthen this important trait. There may be instances where some acquaintances become envious of your successful married life. They may even try to create a rift between you and your spouse. This is yet another instance of putting your trust to the test.

3) If there is an argument and you are at fault, then you should apologize to your spouse.

When a couple has an argument, either both are at fault or one person is wrong. Nevertheless, after a brief lull, both people should behave in a normal manner and start talking again. In other words, the person who made a mistake should apologize. If both are wrong, then they should show magnanimity, apologize to each other, and learn from their mistake. Sometimes ego gets in the way, and the person who is at fault will not apologize. Sometimes the other person will apologize first, although that person may not be responsible for the impasse, showing that person's magnanimity. This act is not a weakness; rather, it is a strength.

The matter will intensify if the deadlock is not broken at the earliest opportunity. Letting an issue linger will result in a steady downward course. The couple could begin acting in a nonchalant manner to each other, which could result in further complications. Remember, by apologizing you are not losing your reputation or hurting your ego. In reality, you are displaying your generosity and proving that you have a big heart. Perhaps you value the relationship more than your ego or arrogance. It is normal to argue in a polite way, as long as it does not happen too often and you reach a conclusion together. If both of you have too much pride, then nobody wins.

4) Love should take precedence over money and material things.

Despite your demanding job, always make a point to spend quality time with your family in the evening. By and large, the entire family should have evening meals together at home. Dedicate Saturdays to family events, unless something else important comes up. Entrepreneurs sometimes work during the weekends, so they should compensate for the lost family time, maybe during the weekdays. Go on mini-vacations with your family and friends. Spend one-on-one time with your spouse and your kids. Participate in family sports events, help kids with their homework or projects, and teach new life skills to them. If you give it some serious thinking, you can come up with innovative ideas for engaging with the family.

If you have genuine love for your spouse and family and they reciprocate it, you will experience peace and equanimity. This will reinforce the inner joy and peace that will help you in pursuing the work of your liking. This will automatically translate into more money and financial security. You will not have to chase money; the money will chase you. Nevertheless, your job skills and your performance are just as important for your professional success. Instead, if you hanker after money and keep thinking about money all the time, you will spend an enormous amount of time at work. You might achieve a lot of financial success, but your family life will take its toll. Perhaps your spouse is more interested in your time or your kids want to engage with you more often. You need to decide for yourself what is important for you. Are you willing to strike a balance between your professional life and your personal life? Remember, as you climb to the top of the echelon in your career, you will have more responsibilities at work and less time for your family. So you will have to determine how you will make up for the lost family time.

5) Put the interests of your family first, and then think about benevolence and social causes.

There is a saying, "Charity begins at home." You should be sure your family is taken care of before you use needed resources for others. Ideally, by the time you retire you will have no mortgage or other debt. Provide basic necessities of life to your wife, your kids, and your extended family. Set up a living irrevocable trust fund for your loved ones. You can place some of your valuable assets into your trust, like real estate, stocks, cash, jewelry, and so on. It would be better to set up a meeting with an attorney, select your beneficiaries, and set stipulations for disbursements. Once you have taken care of your family, you can then do something for society and be generous to people who are not as fortunate as you are.

Sometimes some people who have a great passion for serving humanity go overboard in their pursuits of benevolence at the expense of their own family. For example, they might try to cut corners on providing some extra luxuries to their spouse or children. They may live an ascetic life at home and not allow themselves worldly comforts. They do this because they genuinely want to do something for the disadvantaged. If some calamity strikes the family around that time (say, a major health issue), it could in fact have an impact on the rest of the family. So plan your work and work your plan.

6) Love yourself in an unconditional way.

Assume that you are all alone somewhere. During this time, "you" are the only thing you have. You should love your own company during these moments. Experience that deep love for yourself from the inside first and know yourself better; only then will it manifest from the outside. Make yourself aware of your own unique and powerful qualities and start liking them on a regular basis. But how will you negate some of your weaknesses? That will happen when your family, friends, and acquaintances give you unconditional acceptance, along with some self-analysis and a little improvement on your shortcomings. However, you should spend the majority of your time on further enhancing your strengths, and less time on improving your weaknesses, in particular when it comes to work. If you spend a major portion of your time in improving your weaknesses, you will have a burnout.

Do not confuse self-love with narcissism and berating people around you. I am making this statement with a different connotation. When you love your own self, you will take every action to keep yourself in good hands. One of the powerful motivational factors would be that you would love to be fit and energetic for the sake of your family. After all, you will have that feeling in your mind that you love your family, and for their sake you have to remain fit because you do not want to inconvenience them with any major sickness. It again translates into loving your own self first and developing meaningful relationships.

7) Give respect to your spouse and kids, especially in front of relatives and friends.

If you have become a role model for an ideal family, people will willingly appreciate you for that. Talking and acting in a courteous manner with your spouse and kids in a social gathering will give a boost to your image. People will notice it and they would love to learn from you about family and relationships.

People judge you by your actions and they will judge you by the way you treat your spouse and kids in their presence. Showing mutual respect to each other in front of others will gain you more popularity. You will be considered a role model, and people will want to follow your example.

8) Respect your spouse's parents and relatives.

There are endless possibilities by which you can show that you care for your spouse's parents. Unless they live in the same household, you should visit each other or talk over the phone at times. Once in a while you may take vacations together, give gifts, be with them at times of need, and assist them, especially when they are sick. Sometimes you should place a call to your spouse's relatives. This way there will be a bonding between the two families.

There is a saying that actions are louder than words. You have to show, through your actions, that you care for your spouse's family. This small act will increase the connection between you and your spouse. Your spouse will respect you for your attitude and thinking. However, if you pass disparaging remarks (on purpose or by mistake) about your spouse's parents in front of your family or friends, it will negatively affect your relationship.

9) If a relationship starts drifting apart, try your best to heal it fast by massive self-analysis and retrospection.

Do some contemplation and try to find out what went wrong. If it is your fault, then make a sincere apology. Try to communicate in an open manner, listen, do not get defensive, and if you have to talk, give a gentle smile and talk in a low tone. If you start yelling or try to hush the other person, most of the time you will not have any control over your words. You might make a disparaging comment that you may regret later. In essence, you have to keep your ego at bay. And remember, to err is human. If you accept your mistakes, you have a decent chance of fixing a relationship that is drifting apart.

When a relationship starts drifting apart due to various reasons, the first thing that becomes impacted is communication. Couples communicate less with each other and they start showing a lot of indifference. If this trend continues, they do not share intimate moments with each other. It also has an impact on their physical and mental well-being. These are some signs of fissures developing in a relationship.

10) A lot of people want to win all the time.

You have to accept a universal truth that you cannot win in life all the time. Life is full of peaks and valleys, where peaks are your good times and valleys are your bad times. You do not have to win every time, and if you see merit in your spouse's argument, accept it and apologize. If you do not, then that means you are egoistic and you will start having internal squabbles within the family. If you do apologize, that means you are not arrogant and are down to earth.

Just as one sees vicissitudes in her career and health, the same logic applies to relationships. One of the fundamental reasons some relationships turn bitter is that people want to win all the time. This means that sometimes, even if your spouse is right, you still will choose not to accept it because you want to win the argument and not hurt your ego.

11) Have open and friendly relations with your kids.

Be open, understanding, and friendly with your children. Reinforce the habit of being honest and always speaking the truth. Let them know that if they make a mistake and are truthful about it, they will not be punished. However, if they are dishonest, tell lies, and withhold information that parents should know, then there will be consequences.

Treat your kids as friends, respect some of their opinions about certain things, understand them, and sometimes try to think from their perspective. In this way, you develop a strong and trustworthy relationship with them. They will not need to hide anything from you and they will always be open to talk about whatever may be bothering them. As parents, it is our responsibility to always learn about parenting and inculcate good moral values in our kids. Do not try to act as a strict disciplinarian or as a very lenient parent. Just strike a balance between the two extremes.

12) Set aside some time for reflecting on improving your relationships.

Occasionally set aside some time, in complete solitude, to ponder upon the health of your relationship with your family. Ask questions about what has worked in the past and what has not worked. Learn from your mistakes, and try not to repeat those mistakes for a more fulfilling family life. Think about new ways and techniques by which you can make your relationship stronger.

When you reflect upon the health of your relationship on a periodic basis and in complete solitude, you become more self-aware and mature.

You will get new ideas and ways of how to behave in a particular situation.

13) If you have a demanding job and have a bad day at work, do not vent your frustration on your spouse and kids when you are back home.

Even if you already had a stressful day at work, you should reboot your brain and elevate your mood the moment you arrive home. Greet your family with a big smile and many hugs. It will only take a few minutes to do this. After exchanging pleasantries, you should sit down and relax for a few moments. It is imperative that your spouse and kids not barrage you with questions and complaints the minute you step into the house. All of you should give one another some time to unwind, and unfold the day's events gradually. This will have a tremendous change in the mood of your spouse, and a healthy conversation will begin.

After a bad day at work, if you vent your frustration on your family, it will have a bad effect on their mood. There will be stress and anxiety all around you.

14) Share lessons from life that you have learned over time with your children.

Block some time once in a while for your kids and share lessons with them that you have learned from life. This activity has to start when the kids are young, as their brains are still developing, and it should continue as they get older. At a young age, kids are nonjudgmental and anything you put in their brain will reflect in their personality as they get older. In order for the conversation to be quite effective, share your own real-life stories and stories of others with them. You should also create emotions during these stories. Be a good and effective storyteller so your kids will be moved by your stories; this will help create a lasting impact on them.

Remember, a child who lives with ridicule learns to be diffident and a child who lives with denigration learns to condemn others. Likewise, a child who lives with antagonism learns to be hostile and jealous. However, kids who live with knowledge (which you provide them with at a young age) learn wisdom, and kids who live with happiness will find immense love and beauty as they get older. They will also learn how to be considerate if they see you caring for others within and outside of the family.

15) It is all right to argue at times without worrying about its impact on a healthy relationship.

If an argument cannot be avoided, we should make certain that we maintain a healthy demeanor. Be sure that the discussion does not get bogged down with unnecessary detail or go off on a tangent. If something like that happens, we should stop the argument right away.

If we do not have a healthy disagreement on some occasions, then it means we do not care much about each other. That is the difference between a healthy argument and a cantankerous argument that proves detrimental in the end. Sometimes, some healthy arguments happen out of love and caring.

16) The most appropriate time to communicate your point is when your spouse is in a good disposition.

Look for a time when your spouse is in a happy mood. You have a better chance of putting your point forward and getting a favorable response.

If you have to say something important or convince your spouse or your kids of something, check their mood first. It is very likely that they will not give their undivided attention to you or care about what you have to say if they are in a grumpy mood. When a person is grouchy, his listening power and his patience are short lived.

17) Ask open-ended questions and minimize closed-ended questions during important conversations.

The best approach to break the ice during an impasse is by asking a lot of open-ended questions. You need to flip the questions to your spouse or kids to pick their brain, such as asking, "What do you think you would do in such-and-such situation?" Another question could be, "How can we make this relationship more meaningful and long-lasting?" When you get an answer, do not be defensive; just listen. Also, from time to time, we should remind each other that since we did X, that is why we got Y results.

When we give an opportunity to another person to express her views, she feels that her opinions are valued within the family. In turn, your listening and giving respect will also ensure that everyone within the family will value the opinions of one another.

18) Minimize parenting disagreement by advance planning.

You should discuss your parenting plans with your spouse well in advance and in private. Make sure the kids are not listening to your conversation. This way you will have a united front and the children will not be able to play one parent against the other if you have to discipline them.

There could be a disagreement between you and your spouse about disciplining children. Sooner or later it might result in open arguments in front of the kids. This is not good for you or the kids.

19) Laugh often within the family. It is very good for the kids as they grow up.

Laugh often within the family. Tell jokes to each other and watch funny movies. Hang out with people who have a good sense of humor. Whenever possible, take your kids to social gatherings so that they can connect with other kids. During weekends, go out for day picnics with friends who have kids of similar ages to your own. Also, do not be afraid to laugh at yourself if you make a silly mistake in front of kids.

If you have a good sense of humor, it will have a direct bearing on your kids. They will also develop these traits as they get older. If you are more social and funny, they will in all likelihood develop that personality. If you have a serious disposition and like solitude and loneliness, chances are that your kids will perhaps become like that when they get older. The more exposure you give to your children at big gatherings and social events, the more confident and assertive they will become. However, this process has to start when your kids are young, as you are feeding their brains with the joy of being among people.

20) Compliment your spouse and kids in an openhearted manner when they do something nice.

You can say something like, "Wow! That was great, so nice of you, really appreciate your concern, thank you for being around during tough times, you are awesome, you are the best." The list goes on and on. Show some creativity here and come up with your own compliments.

It is natural that people want to be appreciated and valued. It feels good and it enhances the bonding within the family. Genuine compliments enhance individuals' confidence level. This is true with kids in particular. Children who live with praise learn to appreciate. If they live with affection, they learn to love; and if they live with encouragement, they learn confidence.

21) Sometimes it is a good idea to end a relationship with difficult people altogether and move on in life, since it means you might have hit a roadblock.

Part ways on a good note with those kinds of people. You do not have to be nasty before unfriending them. It is not your job to mend their ways or make them realize their repeated mistakes. You are simply wasting your time and energy. You are better off forgetting about those people and moving on with your life.

Do not keep grudges against people who did something wrong to you. Apparently, you are just exhausting your mental energy while those people have nothing to lose. You may not know, but the truth is that they may not be thinking as much about you as you think they are. Besides, some people enjoy feeling jealous or trying to harm others. Without a doubt, you do not want to be one of those people.

22) Choose your friends with care and have a few unpretentious and loyal friends.

People often attract other people who share common interests with them and in whose presence they feel comfortable and happy. It is like getting that epiphany that says, "Yes, this is the person whom I should be friends with."

Sometimes you meet these special people when you still a child. In other cases you find those friends as you transition into adolescence or adulthood and maybe even in old age. You develop that trust and bonding because you have tested those people, especially during your bad times. Based on your experience, you find that they can do anything for you without feeling bad for themselves. In that friendship, there are no formal rules and no give-and-take attitude. You just share pure self-effacing care and a genuine demeanor.

Fortunate are those people who have a few close and true friends who are by their side through thick and thin, like a rock. Those people are not opportunists or sycophants who are only around during good times. They are not judgmental, and they do not say bad things about you behind your back. They just accept you the way you are. Sometimes they will give you genuine feedback about yourself (whether solicited or not), because they indeed care for you. In case of an adversity, they will put everything aside to be by your side. If you have a few true friends, they will be your pillar of emotional and mental strength. However, those kinds of friends only come in a handful, not in dozens.

A short note to end this chapter:

Remember, life is short and you never know what is going to happen in the next moment. The past is history and the future is a mystery. Nevertheless, you have total control over the present moment. It is in your hands to make this particular moment an awesome one, and this holds true in relationships as well. Forgive people who did something wrong to you and do not hold any grudges against anybody. If you did something wrong to anybody, apologize with total sincerity. Remember, nicer people have more friends and unlikeable people have fewer friends.

Chapter Five: Finances and Retirement Planning

"You can retire from a job, but do not ever retire from making extremely meaningful contributions in life."
–Stephen Covey

Start your retirement planning at a young age and be farsighted about your financial stability after your retirement. I cannot overstress the importance of this concept. You need to think ahead of time and come out with an action plan for your retirement. That action plan should include finances as well as how you are going to spend your days once you retire.

When you are young, visualize what your days will be like once you become old. In other words, try to fast-forward your life several decades into the future and see that picture. Does it give you pain or pleasure? If it gives you pain, based on your current situation, then you have a lot of work to do. If it gives you pleasure, then you are on your way to having a terrific living after retirement. Either way, you have to keep those checks and balances in your financial or retirement planning. In fact, maintaining a journal and writing about your retirement and financial goals will do wonders. Besides, you can edit the journal, whether in electronic form or in paper form, whenever the need arises. By writing your financial and retirement goals, you are reinforcing this information in your subconscious brain, which will help you tremendously in making those goals a reality. You should try to save at least 20% of your earnings for your retirement. Having substantial savings for your retirement will give you peace of mind. You will not have to live on government sops or be at the mercy of your friends and family. Besides, you will earn your respect in the society. If you can save a little more, that is even better. Nevertheless, everybody's situation is different, and not all of the following tips will be applicable to every individual. However, it is a good idea to stay well informed on this crucial subject. So here are some tips on finances and retirement.

1) Pay off your home before you retire for peace of mind.

If you buy a house in your early years of employment, you may have paid off your mortgage by the time you retire. Even if you change jobs and move to different cities or different states, it is possible in most cases. For example, by making two additional mortgage payments every year to your lender, you will be able to repay your mortgage well ahead of the mortgage term length.

Pay your house in full before you retire. You will have the satisfaction that you have your own place to live and will not have to worry about any monthly mortgage payments. You will only be paying your property taxes and homeowners' association dues for maintaining common areas.

2) Save for your children's college education.

Start a 529 education savings plan for your kids for their college education as quickly as you can. The state where you live does not affect these plans. For example, you may start a 529 plan in California and send your kids to a college or university in New York. If you choose not to open a 529 account, you may start a savings account and deposit a fixed amount of money into it every month for your kids' higher education.

With proper planning, when it is time to send your kids to college, you will not have to worry too much about tuition. Even if your kids have to take out a student loan for their college education, it will not be a humongous amount. Your saving for your kids' education will offset some of the loan amount. Besides 529 plans are tax-advantaged accounts designed especially for college savings.

3) Don't buy snazzy cars and expensive gadgets.

Ask yourself whether you really need these things. You could buy a gadget that costs less than the competition, but it can still have the same features and benefits that are important to you. In many instances, we buy gizmos because we want to create a status symbol. That same logic applies to buying snazzy convertible cars. Do your math and see if you can afford the monthly payments or the high costs of maintenance of these cars. You should not have buyer's remorse after the fact.

If you cannot afford or will not use a high-tech electronic gadget, do not buy it. The same logic applies to snazzy cars and luxury goods. Technology is changing so fast that an expensive gadget will become old-fashioned in no time anyway. However, it is okay to go overboard and buy some luxury goods sometimes if that makes you happy, but do not overdo it. After all, you will save some money if you resist unwary buying habits.

4) Open a savings account for your own continuing education.

Put about 5% of your income into your continuing-education savings account. Spend the money that you accrue in this account on gaining knowledge, wisdom, and education throughout your lifetime. Do not consider this money as an expense; it is an investment.

With continuing education, you will think better and make more-informed decisions in your personal and professional life. This small investment will pay itself in no time by increasing your earning potential. Just be sure to apply the knowledge you gain in your day-to-day activities.

5) Open a savings account for post-retirement health expenses.

Set aside about 5% of your income in a Health Savings Account. This money will pay for any medical or pharmacy deductibles, if a situation arises. This is in addition to your private health insurance coverage or some public health programs like Medicare.

Life is so unpredictable. Despite your best efforts, things happen. Are you prepared for any unforeseen health issues at a later part of your life? People become critically sick all of a sudden and need to be hospitalized. Remember, the money that you have saved in the Health Savings Account will come in handy in those difficult and possibly expensive situations.

6) Open a savings account for emergency purposes.

Put 5% of your income into a savings account meant for emergency purposes. However, there is a catch. Even if you put money in this account every month, you have to forget that this account exists. You can set up automatic payments from your checking account into this account and then forget about it.

Life throws a lot of curves at us. Sometimes a situation could arise when you might be in desperate need of some money and you might have exhausted all other means. This savings account could come to your rescue at that time. This is what we call "money saved for a rainy day."

7) Open a savings account for travel and vacation.

Put another 5% of your monthly earnings into a travel and vacation savings account. Again, the catch is that you have to assume this account does not exist at all. The idea is to train your brain that there is nothing in this account.

This account will accrue substantial money over a period of time. You can utilize these funds for some travel and leisure activities after retirement. This will ensure that you will not have to give up your periodic travel and vacation plans due to economic reasons.

8) Know your Social Security benefits.

Check with the Social Security Administration about your benefits. Make sure you check the annual statements that are now available online to get an idea of your eligibility. You will receive Social Security benefits so long as you qualify. Essentially, you may begin to take your benefits at age 62 as long as you do not earn more money than allowed by the Social Security Administration. If you are still working full time, you should wait until full retirement age (approximately 66 years old or even older). If you do not qualify for benefits in your own account, you may be entitled to receive half of your spouse's benefits; this is in addition to your spouse receiving all of his own benefits.

The Social Security Trust funds are not going to last forever, unless the US Treasury changes the regulations. This is also the case with the

Medicare Hospital Trust fund and the Disability Insurance Trust fund as well.

9) Diversify your portfolio.

If you have some residual income, invest in your 401K plan, IRA, stocks and bonds, mutual funds, international investments, etc. Talk to some of your trusted friends and ask for some references for good financial advisors. After doing your research, work with a financial advisor and explore some of the best options based on your financial situation.

You should not put all of your savings into one type of investment, as the risks of something going wrong are substantial. It is important to spread your money around in multiple investments so that a setback in one may be offset by other investments.

10) Downsize your home in a good housing market in anticipation of your retirement.

If you purchased a big house when you were young because of family considerations (for example, because you had children at home or maybe because you were caring for aging parents), you should consider downsizing your home after you plan to retire. Then, if you sell your existing house and buy a smaller one, you can invest the differential money in a portfolio that can have a good return on investment. With this return on investment, for example, you may buy a small vacation home at a place where you would love to spend a few months every year. It is better to have two small homes in different cities rather than having one big home.

By downsizing your home, you will earn some equity and save a significant amount of money. A small home or condominium will save you some money on utilities, property taxes, and homeowners' association dues. Besides, a small single-story home will be easier to clean and maintain during old age. If you own a vacation home in a warm climate, for instance, you may spend a few months in that home when it is much colder in your hometown. Keeping away from extreme cold and snow for a few months every year is good for your bones and skin.

11) Become a student and a teacher.

Now is the time to learn that new language you always wanted to learn but did not have enough time in the past to pursue. This is also a perfect time to teach people about something you are passionate about. Be constantly on the lookout for exploring new things and having an inquisitive mind. You should never be ashamed of putting questions about your areas of interest to experts in those fields.

If you develop a lifelong-learning mindset, you will always have a thirst for knowledge and wisdom. You will be full of life and energy, as you will always be exploring new avenues of learning. There will be an innate feeling that you have limited time in this world but so many things to do. This will develop a deep sense of urgency in your mind, and you will also understand the value of time.

12) Start a meetup group in your hometown.

There are websites like www.meetup.com where you can start a group and invite people. Individuals with similar interests meet regularly at a designated place. They take part in group activities or sports, are part of a support group and help one another in a myriad of areas.

This is a great way of making new friends and connections. You socialize regularly, which keeps you healthy and lifts your mood. You may volunteer your time for some activity, or find a gig where you earn some money.

13) Lead an active life after retirement by planning your day ahead of time.

Once you retire, you should get into the habit of making a list of everything that you are planning to do tomorrow. You should make these lists one day in advance, and they should include activities such as walking, reading, exercising, eating healthy foods, and socializing with family and friends. Other activities could include meditation and relaxation, writing, brain games, and puzzles. These are just a few examples; you should create your own list of activities.

After retirement, if people do not lead an active life and do not keep themselves busy throughout the day, they start ruminating over the past. They start developing an inner guilt about things that went wrong in their life or things they could have done differently. However, if you keep yourself busy the whole day, you will have less time to think about "what might have been." This will improve your mental and emotional energies—in other words, you will have better health. Besides, by planning your day in advance, you will utilize your time better and monitor the activities at the end of the day.

14) Keep working a few hours a day even if you have a sound financial backup after retirement.

You can take a small part-time job in your area of expertise. For example, if you love reading and writing, you can start writing articles, blogs, books, etc. If you love to travel, you can write travelogues. Just think about an area where you have tremendous passion and you want to do something about it. Remember, you may or may not eventually aim for making more money along the way. You are simply doing this to provide a tonic for your brain.

Some people think that they have worked extremely hard their entire life and have earned a lot of money, and now the time has come to relax and enjoy life after retirement. So they may be leading an active lifestyle, but they may not be challenging their brain to maintain their cognitive skills. That is why it is important to stay engaged in a small job or activity that will challenge your brain and compel you to think intelligently. In this way, you will start developing new neural connections in your brain, and this will help prevent brain-related ailments, like dementia and Alzheimer's.

15) Move to a state that is retirement friendly.

Plan in advance and research moving to another state that is more tax friendly for retirees. You also have to keep your quality of life in mind while making a decision. States like North Dakota, South Dakota, Tennessee, Louisiana, Virginia, West Virginia, and Mississippi offer a lower cost of living, lower tax burden, affordable access to healthcare, more affordable houses, and good recreation.

Moving to smaller cities and towns has a lot of advantages once you retire. There are fewer people living in smaller cities, which means that you can find more open spaces, less-crowded malls, and less traffic on the roads. The cost of living is considerably lower than in big cities and metropolitan areas. The air quality is much better compared to big cities, also. In fact, the benefits are numerous. So think about considering this as an option.

16) Move to another country after retirement for a lower cost of living.

If you have friends and relatives overseas, talk to them to get an idea about the cost of living in another country. Do your own research and find out all the pros and cons of living in a foreign country after retirement. Research the quality of primary and critical medical care, including buying medical insurance and the deductibles involved. Also, do research about how you are going to lead an active life in a country overseas.

Some people would love to live in a foreign country after retirement, for numerous reasons. Perhaps they have some family in a foreign country, or the cost of living is much lower there. Another reason could be lower healthcare expenses, which is very important to most people.

A short note to end this chapter:

Imagine a post-retirement life where you are leading a healthy lifestyle with your better half—a life full of energy, happiness, enthusiasm, and a sense of accomplishment. Then, when it is time to say goodbye to this world, you have a deep sense of satisfaction and a smile on your face with little or no regrets. It is possible to do that, but you have to start working on it very early in life. Sometimes, due to lack of experience or being too opinionated, we mess around during our lives; that can have some far-reaching implications for our lives in our old age. Do not let that happen to you. You can turn around your life at any time, if you have a resolute mind and a firm belief in your capabilities.

Chapter Six: Communication and Influencing Skills

"The most important thing in communication is hearing what isn't said."
–Peter Drucker

Here are the three components of communication. The message to be conveyed (Verbal), the tonality of voice (Vocal), and the body language (Visual). These three parts of communication should blend with each other proportionately to convey our emotions and feelings with greater impact. In other words, if you want to communicate with ease and not get stilted, put high emphasis on the words you say, how you say it, and your body language. Besides, take an authentic interest in the other person and your level of camaraderie and effectiveness will increase dramatically.

Our quality of communication also depends on our disposition during conversation. If we are happy, energetic, and joyful, we can communicate with ease and conviction. We should continually learn new techniques and methods to improve our communication and influencing skills by reading books, asking questions, watching people communicate with one another, and analyzing all of this. Learn how to communicate with difficult people without giving up your soul, so it is a win-win situation for everybody. Here are some tips that will help you improve your communication skills and make an impact in the other person's mind.

1) Build your vocabulary to communicate more effectively.

Make it a personal goal to learn a few new words every day. You can find great words in the newspaper, your favorite blog, an e-newsletter, a digital or print dictionary, online or print books, or a thesaurus. Check out the newest software to download and learn at your own pace.

With a powerful vocabulary, you express yourself more clearly and articulate your meaning with greater clarity. If you write, your words will flow more smoothly and have a greater impact on your audience. Stronger writing also transforms your work and expands your thinking.

2) Learn a new language.

Learning a new language can be exciting, driven by curiosity and enthusiasm. Deep inside each of us is that desire to do more. Language studies are available through local colleges, online programs, and audio or video programs. You can also expose yourself to a television or radio station of a particular language and read some good books that teach you that language. There are some great products available from companies like Duolingo, Rosetta Stone, and Pimsleur.

Learning a new language allows you to engage in conversations with people who speak that other language. Your brain processes new words and actively improves the way you think, bringing new ideas for handling daily tasks and opportunities.

3) Build your portable digital library with eBooks written by leading public speakers, communicators, influencers, and decision makers.

Today it is easy to build a library of quality books on your favorite topics leveraging eBooks on your smartphone, tablet like an iPad or a computer. Technology is constantly making it easier to synchronize your library and accounts on multiple devices, so you can carry your library everywhere.

Whether you are sitting at a local Starbucks having a Frappuccino, or taking the train for your daily commute, you can observe how other communicators connect personally and professionally. It will give you a deep understanding of how to connect with those around you in all settings. We have become a connection economy, bonded within a global community through technology and Internet communication. Create your competitive edge, integrating technology to broaden your mind, and stay updated on the constantly changing world around you.

4) Be a good listener.

Good listening, often called active listening, is scarce these days. It requires you to listen to the other person without interrupting him and to pay total attention to what he is saying. When it is your turn to speak, make your point, so the other person knows you have heard what he has said and then keep going.

One of the biggest challenges in listening is not hearing what the other person has said. No one wants to talk with someone who pretends to listen but does not hear a thing you have said. Nothing is more deflating. God gave us two ears and one mouth. We should listen more and talk less. You will be surprised how much ground you will cover by being a good listener. Besides, when you listen, you are in a better frame of mind to respond as you get time to think, compose, and rephrase your message.

5) Yelling at someone will not make your point and is not convincing.

To convey a powerful message to a person who is difficult to deal with, talk to her when she is in a good mood and when you are not frustrated. Present your point in a clear, level voice with a smile on your face and wait for her reaction. If she becomes agitated again, stay calm, let her rant, and then explain why you presented your feedback to bring clarity to the situation.

When we engage in an angry argument, we raise our voice to be heard and to dominate or intimidate the other person, so we have an upper edge in the conversation. However, during an angry argument, most people lose their sense of judgment; they often say something in a fit of rage they later regret. Stay calm and command the situation through a controlled, focused voice and message. This conveys the message despite the anger and fitful outbursts.

6) Make a short pause your best answer to a disagreement or before you respond to a contentious issue.

How often has someone asked you a silly question or made a wrong statement? And no matter what you say, it will not change that person's perception of the idea or concept. In these situations, you may be better off using a pregnant pause before responding or simply not responding at all. If you quickly respond to his smirk or a sarcastic statement, you may be prolonging the discussion with unnecessary detail or long-winded, empty conversation.

Using a brief pause creates a moment of thinking, perhaps weakening the comment or allowing the other individual to realize his error or misstatement. Responding after a brief pause may have a stronger effect with a better outcome. You are better off focusing your energy on something more productive and fun than by prolonging a conversation bound for nowhere.

7) Mirror your body language with the other person.

Have you ever noticed that when you start a conversation with another person, you somehow find a common ground to connect? Many times, without thinking, you engage in conversation with someone based on his body language, which usually tells you he is open to talking with you. Once you begin talking, watching his eyes, movements, and other body language helps you dig deep to discover common interests and likings that you share. You may even want to mirror the other person's gestures; for example, if the person leans forward to talk, then you do the same. If he uses certain voice intonations, you do the same. Make sure to include a brief pause between your mutual actions and do not overdo it; if he feels that you are mimicking him, it could have a totally opposite effect.

This is one of the best ways to build instant rapport with the other person and have a meaningful conversation. If the individual believes you are truly interesting and engaging, you will create an indelible imprint within the other person's mind. Your takeaway will leave him smiling instead of regretting bumping into you.

8) Let your body language emanate confidence.

Push your shoulders back and lift your spine with your main torso, and your body will project a look of confidence and assurance. In fact, you may convince yourself that you are sure of what you are saying. An effective technique when speaking publicly is periodically walking away from the lectern and across the podium. This way you address the entire group, not just those directly in front of you.

Standing tall is physiologically good for you. It gives you an extra boost of energy and confidence, which you will emit to the audience. Breathing deeply helps keep you energized and better able to articulate your words and convey their meaning. In point of fact, sometimes a speaker may be afraid the audience will not like his speech, but his body language will never give that message.

9) First understand, then be understood.

Today, society promotes a lot of self-centeredness and entitlement, conveying the message that "I'm more important than you are." Yet if you truly want to make a lasting impression and influence others, gain a deeper understanding, and develop long-lasting relationships, you need to focus on the person in front of you. If your audience (whether a single person or a roomful of people) believes that you are engaged with them, they will respond with greater satisfaction. For example, when your friend meets you, your first inclination will be to talk about your own challenges and problems. It is human nature that people want to talk about themselves and their conundrums more than genuinely listening to other people and their challenges. Instead, ask them how they are doing, inquire about their welfare and any challenges they are facing, and offer some help. Then the door will open for your own issues and difficulties.

By showing your interest in others despite your own difficulties, you are showing them that you truly care about them, even in tough times. This opens the door to greater caring and makes an indelible impact on their mind. They will feel that they can count on you, and some of them will become your lifelong allies.

10) Talk to the person next to you as if he is six feet away from you.

When you want to talk to the person beside you, do so with a calm disposition. Sit relaxed and address that person as if he is six feet away from you, even though you might be sitting just three feet away.

Projecting yourself a little louder than normal will make you feel more confident and assertive and will more likely engage the listener. Today's professionals know that speaking in a very thin and shallow voice depicts a lack of self-assurance and timidity. It reflects that you are not a decision maker but more of a follower, and your decisions may be shallow and somewhat empty. Showing self-confidence and enthusiasm makes it more inviting for others to talk with you. That way, you both share in the enthusiasm and fun.

11) Build your vocal presentation daily to improve the vocal inflections that project during a formal talk.

Whether you employ a voice coach or train yourself through online research and practice in front of a mirror, you will discover areas where your vocal projection needs work and the inflections need perfecting. To change your vocal inflections, change the pitch of your voice when you talk in certain social situations. Try to convey emotion in your voice without changing your demeanor. Record yourself and listen to what you sound like as you read a prepared script. You will hear where you are weak and what areas need practice. Stand in front of a mirror and practice at least once a day, growing to perhaps two or three ten-minute practices a day. As you hear yourself and watch yourself, you will see a change in your self-confidence and how you convey words and ideas through vocal inflection. Keep the older audio files to refer back to when you have gotten better, to see and hear the changes. You will be surprised at your progress within just a few days, weeks, and months.

The best way to improve as a formal speaker is to practice and learn what you do and how to do it better. If you have heard monotone speakers, you know they lose your attention quickly. Stop yourself from sounding like that by practicing, learning how to convey your ideas, and using your voice to project the emotions you want your audience to feel. Once you have captured their attention and held it, they are yours.

12) Keep a pleasant smile on your face when you converse.

Before you speak, put a gentle smile on your face and show a lot of interest and enthusiasm to the other person. Most people love to be around happy people or people who make them laugh and are less judgmental.

Some people believe that we use fewer facial muscles when we smile, and we use more muscles when we are infuriated. Smiles are communicated consciously or subconsciously, and they are treated as a sign of kindness. On the other hand, frowns are considered to be an indication of sadness or disapproval.

13) Leave others in a better disposition than you find them.

Go out of your way to help someone, and the chances are they will do the same for you when needed. If you want to win new friends, think about new and different ways to have meaningful and long-lasting relationships. You need to add new meaning and value to your relationships every time you have a conversation.

If you learn this art, people will always try to be in your company. They will get meaningful value from every conversation that they have with you. They will think that you are a charismatic person who radiates confidence and that every conversation gives some value to them.

14) Maintain proper eye contact when you speak.

Whenever you are conversing, make sure you look into the other person's eyes. However, here is a note of caution. You should gaze at the other person's eyes for just a few seconds and then shift your eyes sideways or somewhere else. After a few more seconds, again look in the other person's eyes while talking. If you feel uncomfortable looking directly in the eyes, then you should look at the other person's nose.

When you look into another person's eyes, it has some advantages. First, the other person feels that you are paying attention and are engaging with him. If you keep your eyes down while talking to a person, it means either you lack confidence or you are hiding something. Besides, it also shows that you are not listening to the other person attentively or you are not giving him much importance.

A short note to end this chapter:

If we communicate in an effective manner at work and home, we can avoid miscommunication and misinterpretation. There will be equanimity at work and at home and you will be one of the most likeable persons at word and play. One of the cardinal secrets of success at work and play is effective communication and influencing skills. You may have seen some people at work who achieve massive success even though they may not have strong job-related skills. These people usually are good communicators. On the other hand, you may know people who are very competent and are highly technical, but they do not have much visibility at work. One of the reasons for this is that they are not very good at communication and cannot express themselves effectively.

Chapter Seven: Philanthropy and Social Cause

"If you help enough people get what they want, you will get what you want."
–Zig Ziglar

How do you feel when you see a homeless person at a traffic signal holding a cardboard sign and wearing shabby clothes on a cold morning? Do you empathize with that person or do you experience some level of sadness? Do you feel like doing something for him? How about a brilliant and smart kid who cannot pursue higher education due to financial difficulties? Perhaps she has the potential to be extremely successful in her life. In addition, how about a person who is lying in a hospital bed for a long time due to a chronic illness?

In these situations, you can perhaps do something about them. A lot depends upon your financial situation and your willingness to be a giver. Sometimes your mere presence at a certain place and in a certain situation could mean a lot to somebody. Giving is a subjective entity and it has wider connotations. Nevertheless, this area may not be applicable to everyone as everybody's situation is different. If this is something that is very close to your heart, then here are some useful tips.

1) Empathize with people who face temporary setbacks.

Sometimes life is running smoothly for somebody and then all of a sudden something dreadful happens. In that case, give emotional and moral support to him in whatever way you can. Do not become overly sentimental about his ordeals for too long. Regardless, you need to have a strong emotional and mental demeanor for your health and success. Also, do not gloat over somebody's misfortune.

When you connect with people at an emotional level, you give them loads of positive energy, which could help them during difficult times. A few kind and empowering words at a rough time might change somebody's life. Your commiseration needs to be genuine, as it will show up in your body language.

2) Help some individuals in their personal and professional development.

Share your valuable life experiences with people around you. Educate people about what works and what does not work in a particular situation. It may be possible that you went through a similar issue in the past. If you have achieved massive success in your career, you may want to share stories about your successes and failures with others.

Your experience and feedback might help people improve their lives and help them grow faster. They might even pay it forward. Maybe your life lessons affect their thinking dramatically, and they get ideas about what works and what does not work in a given situation.

3) Find ways to help your local community.

Devote some time to nonprofit organizations or a social cause that is close to your heart. There are so many foundations and organizations where you can become involved and share your wisdom.

You will experience a deep sense of belonging and fulfillment that you are giving back to society in your own way. You never know when an idea you share with a group of people might solve a lingering problem or create economic opportunities for local communities.

4) Helping others does not always mean monetary support.

You can also help people by giving them your valuable time. That is sometimes harder than helping a person who is in dire financial need. For example, for a very successful and busy executive, time is extremely valuable. However, if the same person takes a hiatus for a few weeks to work for a social cause, that is a very commendable act. This is an excellent example of bequeathing your time rather than your money.

Most people find it hard to part with their time as it is a precious commodity. Every person has only a limited quantity of time available, and every person in this world gets only 24 hours of time in a day.

5) Volunteer within the local schools, rehabilitation centers, and colleges.

If you like public speaking, teaching, or motivating people, you can speak to some regional schools and community colleges and share your life experiences with small kids and youth. Another idea might be to visit a local hospital rehabilitation center to give hope and encouragement to physically challenged patients. You may have to get prior approval from the appropriate authorities, though.

If you are an expert in your field, your expertise might give ideas to the kids or encourage them to perform better in school. When you spend some time with elderly or sick people, and give them hope and positive vibes, you will not only be helping them, but you will get their blessings and perceive a deep sense of joy and internal peace.

6) Develop interest in knowing more about global challenges and connect with like-minded people for bringing social awareness.

Even a casual conversation with an acquaintance will give you some ideas. You could get ideas through reading about problems and challenges faced by others. Even thinking in solitude and jotting down notes will give you some clues about a possible solution to a social issue.

Most people are not mindful about issues and problems faced by others around the globe. We take our life as it comes to us. We can deal with social issues and problems with a resolute mind once we start thinking deeply about them.

7) Start a foundation of your own and bring a few like-minded people on board.

If you create a charitable trust, you can disburse the money to needy people. However, ensure that the money goes to the right person by doing your research. Sometimes, if we are not careful, the money could go to less-deserving individuals. Education and healthcare are some of the important areas where givers can make an immense contribution. Illiteracy is the biggest curse in this world, and if you can do something about it, you are augmenting the Global Human Development Index in your own way one step at a time.

A charitable foundation can go a long way toward improving the standard of living of some people. Besides getting some tax breaks, you are also leaving a legacy behind you. Your benevolence might inspire the beneficiary to do the same for others when the appropriate time comes.

8) Give hope and encouragement to people who feel down and dejected.

Give positive vibes and encouragement to people who think negatively, live in total despair, or are in a constant state of neglect and ridicule. Some of these people might be real gems. Maybe they are living in a negative environment, or are constantly discouraged from taking big steps in their lives.

If you make people realize their potential and help them along the way by giving positive energy and encouragement, those people will probably do the impossible. At the end of the day, you will feel that you improved their lives, and they will consider you a role model.

A small note at the end:

Merely thinking about helping others produces dopamine, a neurotransmitter that controls the brain's gratification centers. There is scientific evidence that people have experienced deep inner joy and a sense of purpose in life by giving to others. It also helps givers increase their own level of happiness and decrease their stress levels. So giving benefits not only the receiver, but the giver as well.

Epilogue

I hope you enjoyed reading this book as much as I enjoyed writing it. However, simply reading the material is not going to do any good unless (and until) you take massive action. You see, there is a difference between knowing something and doing something. Often when we read something inspiring, we get motivated to take action. Therefore, over the next few days we are upbeat about ourselves. Then as time progresses, we start slowing down and eventually go back into our comfort zone. After a while, we again start whining and feeling exasperated. So do not let that happen to you. Constantly remind yourself that you are taking these baby steps as outlined in this book for your own benefit. The fact is that if you work hard right now (sometimes some people think it is a "pain" because there is hard work to do), you will reap the rewards in the future, which is a "benefit" during old age. So start with the tips that are relevant to you and do those exercises.

I wish you all the best for your continued success in your life's journey.

I want to end this book with two quotes.

"The great end of life is not knowledge, but action." –Thomas Huxley

"When you were born you were crying and everyone else was smiling. Live your life so at the end, you are the one who is smiling and everyone else is crying." –Ralph Waldo Emerson

Useful Websites & Books

Here are some useful websites and books that will help you immensely in your tryst towards a fulfilling and purposeful life.

Websites on Thinking and Creativity

www.mindtools.com

www.nightingale.com

www.learningstrategies.com

www.innovationtools.com

www.creativityhacks.com

www.managingthought.com

www.positscience.com

www.lumosity.com

www.fitbrains.com

www.mybraintrainer.com

www.brainbashers.com

www.braingle.com

www.illusions.org

http://cognitivefun.net

Books on Thinking and Creativity

Thinkertoys - A Handbook of Creativity Thinking - Micheal Michalko

Mind Map Book - Tony Buzan

Idea Mapping: How to Access Your Hidden Brain Power - Jamie Nast

What a Great Idea 2.0 - Chic Thompson

Five Star Mind - Tom Wujec

Innovator's Toolkit - David Silverman & Philip Samuel

Awake at the Wheel - Michell Lezis Ditkoff

The Mind Map Book - Tony Buzan

A Kick in the Seat of the Pants - Roger von Oech

Moonwalking with Einstein - Joshua Foer

Thinking, Fast and Slow – Daniel Kahneman

Blink: The Power of Thinking Without Thinking – Malcolm Gladwell

Habit: Why We Do What We Do in Life and Business – Charles Duhigg

Websites on Health and Fitness

www.mayoclinic.com

www.cedars-sinai.edu

www.gaiam.com

www.goodguide.com

www.naturalnews.com

www.yogatoday.com

www.realage.com

www.medicinenet.com

http://nutritiondata.self.com

www.stilltasty.com

http://stresseraser.com

www.yogajournal.com
www.webmd.com
www.medhelp.org
www.healthgrades.com
www.health.com

Books on Health and Fitness

Better Each Day - Jessica Cassity
Eat to Live - Joel Fuhrman
Salt Sugar Fat - Michael Moss
The 4-Hour Body - Timothy Ferriss
Feeling Good – David D. Burns
Mind over Medicine – Lissa Rankin
Spontaneous Healing – Andrew Weil
Healthy Aging – Andrew Weil
Take a Load off Your Heart – Joseph C. Piscatella & Barry A. Franklin
Good Calories, Bad Calories – Gary Taubes
Yoga Cures – Tara Stiles
What to Eat – Marion Nestle
Eat and Run – Mark Lauren

Websites on Career Success

www.hbr.org
www.forbes.com
www.fortune.com
www.linkedin.com

www.hoovers.com

www.indeed.com

www.simplyhired.com

www.glassdoor.com

www.idealist.com

www.wsj.com

www.encore.org

www.transitionsabroad.com

www.workingoverseas.com

www.self-directed-search.com

www.annualreportservice.com

Books on Career Success

Guerrilla Marketing for Job Hunters 3.0 - Jay Conrad Levinson

'Headhunter' Hiring Secrets - Skip Freeman

What Color Is Your Parachute? - Richard N. Bolles

How to Write a KILLER LinkedIn Profile - Brenda Bernstein

The First 90 Days – Michael D. Watkins

The $100 Startup – Chris Guillebeau

Never Eat Alone – Keith Ferrazzi

The 4-Hour Workweek – Timothy Ferriss

What Got You Here, Won't Get You There –Marshall Goldsmith

Who's Got Your Back – Keith Ferrazzi

Websites on Family and Relationships

www.babycenter.com

www.marriagetools.com

www.smartmarriages.com

www.twoofus.org

www.parents.com

www.marriagebuilders.com

www.raisesmartkid.com

Books on Family and Relationships

Men Are from Mars, Women Are from Venus - John Gray

Have a New Teenager by Friday – Kevin Leham

How to Talk So Kids Will Listen & Listen So Kids Will Talk – Adele Faber and Elaine Mazlish

Secrets of Happy Families – Bruce Feiler

The Eight Essential Steps to Conflict Resolution – Dudley Weeks

Wired for Love – Stan Tatkin and Harville Hendrix

The Seven Principles for Making Marriage Work – John Gottman and Nan Silver

The Friendship Factor – Alan Loy McGinnis

Websites on Finances and Retirement

www.aarp.org

www.retirementrevised.com

www.kiplinger.com

www.marketwatch.com

www.investorguide.com

www.mint.com

www.fidelity.com

www.mymoney.gov

www.missingmoney.com

Books on Finances and Retirement

Think and Grow Rich – Napoleon Hill

The Total Money Makeover - Dave Ramsey

How to Retire Happy - Stan Hinden

The Millionaire Next Door – Thomas J. Stanley

You are Broke Because You Want to Be – Larry Winget

Debt-Free Forever – Take Control of Your Money and Your Life – Gail Vaz-Oxdale

The Richest Man in Babylon – George Clason

Rich Dad Poor Dad – Robert Kiyosaki

Websites on Communication and Influencing Skills

www.dalecarnegie.com

www.impactfactory.com

www.toastmasters.org

www.negotiate.org

www.amanet.org

www.ted.com

www.speak-first.com

www.worldbusinessculture.com
www.duolingo.com
www.rosettastone.com
www.pimsleurapproach.com

Books on Communication and Influencing Skills

How to Win Friends & Influence People - Dale Carnegie

Just Listen: Discover the Secret to Getting Through to Absolutely Anyone - Mark Goulston

Power Questions - Andrew Sobel and Jerold Panas

Confessions of a Public Speaker – Scott Berkun

How to Deliver a TED Talk – Jeremey Donovan

Set Your Voice Free - Roger Love

Tell to Win: Connect, Persuade, and Triumph with the Hidden Power of Story - Peter Guber

Crucial Conversations: Tools for Talking When Stakes Are High – Kerry Patterson

The Art of Public Speaking – Stephan Lucas

Website on Philanthropy and Giving

www.charitynavigator.org
www.globalgiving.com
www.wealthengine.com
www.philanthropy.com
www.justgive.org
www.redcross.org
www.kiva.org

Books on Philanthropy and Giving

The Foundation: A Great American Secret - Joel L. Fleishman

Leaving Microsoft to Change the World - John Wood

Giving 2.0 - Laura Arrillaga-Andreessen

Start Something That Matters - Blake Mycoskie

Philanthropy in America - Olivier Zunz

The Ask - Laura Fredricks

About the Author

Arun Thaploo is a business coach, critical thinker, motivational speaker, and sales and marketing expert. His primary role has been in turning around businesses using technology, increasing revenues, and improving people's lives by organizing seminars and workshops on personality development, improving thinking, and creativity.

Arun is a voracious reader who has read thousands of books and has committed himself to lifelong learning. His other areas of interest include music, travel, adventure sports, gardening, and photography. As an ardent traveler, he has been to multiple countries and touched people's lives by understanding human values and emotions. He has a great passion for helping corporations and individuals to explore hidden talent and skills to lead a fulfilling and meaningful life. You can email him at **arun@arunthaploo.com** if the mood strikes you.

Other Title by the Author

This book will give you latest research based and data driven

information about stroke and how to preempt it in most situations.

Here are some of the topics you will learn from this book about stroke and brain damage:

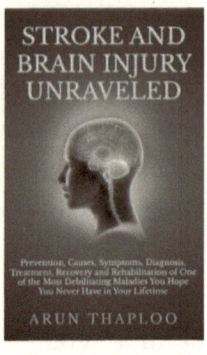

- How to identify if you already might have had a silent stroke in the past, like a TIA stroke without you ever realizing it.

- How to envisage with reasonable accurately whether you are a candidate for an Ischemic stroke or a Hemorrhagic stroke in the future.

- What symptoms should you be vigilant about to understand that you might be having a stroke right now, and what you need to do promptly to prevent significant brain damage?

- How to prevent recurrence of a stroke and what precautions the stroke survivor and family members should take.

- What diagnostics tests should be ordered by your doctor and which tests should not be done on a patient as a result of previous medical history and prevent further complications?

- How family members and caregivers can offer the best care and treatment to a stroke patient at home while taking care of their own emotional, physical and mental wellbeing. And much more.